# ·EXPLORING·

## SCIENCE AND MEDICAL DISCOVERIES

# Atomic Energy

Other books in the
Exploring Science and Medical Discoveries series:

Antibiotics
Cloning
Evolution
Gene Therapy
Germs
Medical Imaging
Space Exploration
Vaccines

# SCIENCE AND MEDICAL DISCOVERIES

# Atomic Energy

Barbara Kanninen, *Book Editor*

Bruce Glassman, *Vice President*
Bonnie Szumski, *Publisher*
Helen Cothran, *Managing Editor*
David M. Haugen, *Series Editor*

**GREENHAVEN PRESS**
*An imprint of Thomson Gale, a part of The Thomson Corporation*

Detroit • New York • San Francisco • San Diego • New Haven, Conn.
Waterville, Maine • London • Munich

| LIBRARY OF CONGRESS CATALOGING-IN-PUBLICATION DATA |
| --- |
| Atomic energy / Barbara Kanninen, book editor. |
| p. cm. — (Exploring science and medical discoveries) |
| Includes bibliographical references and index. |
| ISBN 0-7377-1963-X (lib. : alk. paper) |
| 1. Nuclear engineering. I. Kanninen, Barbara J. (Barbara Joan) II. Series. |
| TK9145.A8253  2006 |
| 621.48—dc22                                    2005045996 |

Printed in the United States of America

# CONTENTS

# Chapter 3: Nuclear Accidents

could occur in the United States, despite safety improvements made since Three Mile Island.

# Chapter 4: Enduring Issues and Controversies

or attack a nuclear power plant, potentially releasing deadly radioactive material into the air.

**M**ost great science and medical discoveries emerge slowly from the work of generations of scientists. In their laboratories, far removed from the public eye, scientists seek cures for human diseases, explore more efficient methods to feed the world's hungry, and develop technologies to improve quality of life. A scientist, trained in the scientific method, may spend his or her entire career doggedly pursuing a goal such as a cure for cancer or the invention of a new drug. In the pursuit of these goals, most scientists are single-minded, rarely thinking about the moral and ethical issues that might arise once their new ideas come into the public view. Indeed, it could be argued that scientific inquiry requires just that type of objectivity.

Moral and ethical assessments of scientific discoveries are quite often made by the unscientific—the public—sometimes for good, sometimes for ill. When a discovery is unveiled to society, intense scrutiny often ensues. The media report on it, politicians debate how it should be regulated, ethicists analyze its impact on society, authors vilify or glorify it, and the public struggles to determine whether the new development is friend or foe. Even without fully understanding the discovery or its potential impact, the public will often demand that further inquiry be stopped. Despite such negative reactions, however, scientists rarely quit their pursuits; they merely find ways around the roadblocks.

Embryonic stem cell research, for example, illustrates this tension between science and public response. Scientists engage in embryonic stem cell research in an effort to treat diseases such as Parkinson's and diabetes that are the result of cellular dysfunction. Embryonic stem cells can be derived from early-stage embryos, or blastocysts, and coaxed to form any kind of human cell or tissue. These can then be used to replace damaged or diseased tissues in those suffering from intractable diseases. Many researchers believe that the use of embryonic stem cells to treat human diseases promises to be one of the most important advancements in medicine.

However, embryonic stem cell experiments are highly controversial in the public sphere. At the center of the tumult is the fact that in order to create embryonic stem cell lines, human embryos must be destroyed. Blastocysts often come from fertilized eggs that are left over from fertility treatments. Critics argue that since blastocysts have the capacity to grow into human beings, they should be granted the full range of rights given to all humans, including the right not to be experimented on. These analysts contend, therefore, that destroying embryos is unethical. This argument received attention in the highest office of the United States. President George W. Bush agreed with the critics, and in August 2001 he announced that scientists using federal funds to conduct embryonic stem cell research would be restricted to using existing cell lines. He argued that limiting research to existing lines would prevent any new blastocysts from being destroyed for research.

Scientists have criticized Bush's decision, saying that restricting research to existing cell lines severely limits the number and types of experiments that can be conducted. Despite this considerable roadblock, however, scientists quickly set to work trying to figure out a way to continue their valuable research. Unsurprisingly, as the regulatory environment in the United States becomes restrictive, advancements occur elsewhere. A good example concerns the latest development in the field. On February 12, 2004, professor Hwang Yoon-Young of Hanyang University in Seoul, South Korea, announced that he was the first to clone a human embryo and then extract embryonic stem cells from it. Hwang's research means that scientists may no longer need to use blastocysts to perform stem cell research. Scientists around the world extol the achievement as a major step in treating human diseases.

The debate surrounding embryonic stem cell research illustrates the moral and ethical pressure that the public brings to bear on the scientific community. However, while nonexperts often criticize scientists for not considering the potential negative impact of their work, ironically the public's reaction against such discoveries can produce harmful results as well. For example, although the outcry against embryonic stem cell research in the United States has resulted in fewer embryos being destroyed, those with Parkinson's, such as actor Michael J. Fox, have argued that prohibiting the development of new stem cell lines ultimately will prevent a timely cure for the disease that is killing Fox and thousands of others.

Greenhaven Press's Exploring Science and Medical Discoveries series explores the public uproar that often follows the disclosure of scientific advances in fields such as stem cell research. Each anthology traces the history of one major scientific or medical discovery, investigates society's reaction to the breakthrough, and explores potential new applications and avenues of research. Primary sources provide readers with eyewitness accounts of crucial moments in the discovery process, and secondary sources offer historical perspectives on the scientific achievement and society's reaction to it. Volumes also contain useful research tools, including an introductory essay providing important context, and an annotated table of contents enabling students to quickly locate selections of interest. A thorough index helps readers locate content easily, a detailed chronology helps students trace the history of the discovery, and an extensive bibliography guides readers interested in pursuing further research.

Greenhaven Press's Exploring Science and Medical Discoveries series provides readers with inspiring accounts of how generations of scientists made the world's great discoveries possible and investigates the tremendous impact those innovations have had on the world.

# INTRODUCTION

**P**rotons and neutrons, the particles found inside an atomic nucleus, are so small it would take 13 trillion of them, lined up in a row, to span an inch. Yet the attraction between these nuclear particles is the strongest natural attraction ever discovered. Breaking their bonds produces a burst of energy that is millions of times more powerful than the energy produced by chemical reactions such as the burning of coal. The idea of so much energy coming from something so small seems almost miraculous. It is no wonder expectations for atomic energy were high in the early years of its discovery and development.

In 1954 Admiral Lewis L. Strauss, chairman of the U.S. Atomic Energy Commission, predicted that atomic energy would produce electricity "too cheap to meter." President Dwight D. Eisenhower, in a speech known as "Atoms for Peace," hoped it would bring prosperity, and therefore peace, to all nations. Since the end of World War II the U.S. government has invested more than a trillion dollars in research and development, nuclear reactor construction, and other activities necessary to get the atomic energy industry up and running.

Given this enormous investment, some critics wonder whether atomic energy has lived up to expectations. The industry itself appears to be stagnating. Electric utilities have not proposed any new nuclear reactors since 1979. The 103 nuclear power plants operating in the United States are all scheduled to be shut down or decommissioned by 2075. At the end of the day, it is not clear that atomic energy has a future in the modern energy marketplace.

The energy market has changed in several ways since atomic energy first became a reality shortly after World War II. First, renewable energy resources have emerged and are becoming more competitive. Second, public awareness and concern over environmental issues—such as the disposal of nuclear waste generated by nuclear power—has grown substantially. Third, the new threat of terrorism has exacerbated public concern about the risk of nuclear power plant accidents. How atomic energy fares with regard to these issues will determine whether it can stay alive as a viable energy option. The most important issue by far, however, is money. Atomic energy must be able to compete head-to-head against traditional fossil fuels, namely coal, and the new, renewable energy resources to produce the cheapest kilowatt-hour (the amount that would power a one-thousand-watt lightbulb for one hour) of electricity. If it cannot do so, it may disappear from the marketplace altogether.

## The Cost of a Kilowatt-Hour

Burning coal generates electricity for a bit less than two cents per kilowatt-hour. Cost estimates for atomic energy vary. Some estimates are as low as one cent per kilowatt-hour, indicating that atomic energy could compete with coal. On the other hand, some estimates go as high as ten cents per kilowatt-hour. Since more researchers lean toward the latter estimates, the majority agree that atomic energy cannot compete.

The wide range in estimates is due to the different assumptions experts have made about which types of costs are, or are not, relevant. For example, the one-cent estimate, which shows atomic energy being cheaper than coal power, only includes costs that would occur *after a nuclear reactor is up and running.* In other words, it ignores the extraordinary up-front cost of atomic energy: the cost of designing, licensing, and constructing a nuclear reactor. As an example, New Hampshire's Seabrook Number 1 facility cost $5.8 billion to get up and running in 1990. Thus, although the energy produced may be inexpensive, the initial investment will increase the cost of that energy. In the words of Dashka Slater of *Sierra* magazine, "Saying nuclear power plants are efficient is a bit like saying moon rocks are free for the taking."[1] Most experts agree that when the cost of building a nuclear reactor is included in the estimate, coal power is cheaper than atomic energy.

This finding is consistent with what the marketplace shows. If atomic energy were in fact cheaper than coal power, electric utilities would want to increase their production of it. They would build more reactors. However, they have not. Either utilities do not have the funds to build such massive projects, or they do not have the interest, or both. When asked if his company would build a new nuclear reactor, the chief executive of Dominion, a Virginia-based energy company, expressed severe reservations. "Standard and Poor's and Moody's would have a heart attack," he said, referring to the agencies that evaluate the debt loads companies carry. "And my chief financial officer, too."[2] In other words, his company could not rationalize atomic energy's extraordinary up-front expense.

Renewable energy sources are also emerging and some may ultimately become cheaper than atomic energy, if they are not already. According to energy consultants and long-time advocates of renewable energy Amory B. Lovins and L. Hunter Lovins:

> Super-efficient gas plants or wind farms cost 5 cents to 6 cents: co-generation of heat and power often 1 cent to 5 cents. The cost of saving a kilowatt-hour through efficient lights, motors and other electricity-saving devices is under 2 cents. They're all getting cheaper. So are the next winners: fuel cells and solar cells—where a pound of silicon can produce more electricity than a pound of nuclear fuel.[3]

Atomic energy advocates argue that atomic energy will also get cheaper when, or if, newer, more efficient reactors are built. Most energy experts, however, still point to coal as the cheapest energy source, both now and in the future.

## The Environmental Question

Though fundamentally important, monetary cost is not the only consideration that matters when determining which energy sources might be most worthy of future investment. The environment, for example, is an important public policy consideration, and the environmental perspective does not look favorably upon coal power.

There is no doubt that the environmental costs of coal-powered electricity are severe. Pollutants emitted by the burning of coal include ozone, volatile organic compounds (VOCs), carbon monoxide (CO), carbon dioxide ($CO_2$), sulfur dioxide ($SO_2$) and nitrogen oxide (NOx). These have been linked to health problems, including exacerbation of asthma and breathing problems, reduced resistance to colds, aging of lung tissue, and reduced ability of the blood to bring oxygen to body cells. Some of these emissions also produce smog, which affects visibility. $SO_2$ disperses in the air, combines with precipitation, and comes back to earth as acid rain, acidifying water and land all over the world. Ozone and $CO_2$ contribute to the greenhouse effect and global warming, a trend that deeply troubles scientists and policy makers and could have enormous impact on human and animal habitats all over the world. In addition, the mining of coal via "strip-mining" is devastating to the land and environment. Coal is not an environmentally friendly energy source, yet it currently provides 54 percent of U.S. electricity.

In contrast, atomic energy—produced by the continual splitting of uranium atoms (fission)—is mostly environmentally benign. A surprisingly small quantity of uranium is used in fission. Nothing is burned, and no VOCs, CO, $CO_2$, $SO_2$, or NOx fumes or particles are emitted. There is no greenhouse effect. From an environmental perspective, atomic energy is clearly superior to coal—in all but one respect. Atomic energy has an environmental Achilles' heel: radioactivity.

## Radioactivity: The Problem That Will Not Go Away

Radioactivity occurs when nuclei come apart—either naturally as with radioactive decay, or artificially as with nuclear fission. Atomic energy cannot be produced without also producing a radioactive by-product: waste. Radioactive waste is poisonous to animals, plants, and humans. It remains potentially deadly for many, many thousands of years. If it is not contained in completely secure, leak-proof storage units for its entire span of existence, it can do extraordinary damage to the surrounding environment, making it uninhabitable for centuries.

Unfortunately, the United States has not found a workable solution to this environmental hazard. The questions of where and how to permanently store radioactive waste are so complex, long-term, and frightening that public-policy makers, for the most part, have found it easier to avoid making specific decisions regarding them. The United States does have a permanent storage facility (almost) ready to begin operating in Yucca Mountain, Nevada. NIMBY ("Not In My Back Yard") grassroots politics, however, continue to prevent it from opening for business. In the meantime, radioactive waste is stored on-site at nuclear plants, in "temporary" containers and pools designed to last about forty years.

Until and unless a safe, permanent storage facility is opened, the radioactive waste issue will remain atomic energy's most contentious problem. It is not, however, its only problem. Closely tied to the radioactive waste issue is the risk of a nuclear power plant accident, or meltdown, which would release deadly radioactive material into the environment. Ever since the 1979 nuclear power plant accident at Three Mile Island, the question of reactor safety has dogged the nuclear power industry.

## The Risk of Meltdown

"Nuclear power-producing units will be dangerous instruments and careful thought will have to be given to their safe construction and operation."[4] Edward Teller, a nuclear scientist who played a significant role in the development of the U.S. atomic bomb, made this statement in a 1953 letter to Sterling Cole, the chair of the Congressional Joint Committee on Atomic Energy. The danger Teller referred to was the risk of a power plant accident.

Since Teller's letter, there have been two large-scale nuclear power plant accidents: the first at Three Mile Island in 1979 and the second at Chernobyl, in the Ukraine, in 1986. In addition, according to the Union of Concerned Scientists, literally thousands of safety issues have cropped up at U.S. nuclear power plants. In the last two decades, for example, twenty-seven plants were shut down for a year or more to deal with safety concerns.

Teller's vision for the development of atomic energy would have focused on building "inherently safe" technologies—that is, technologies designed to be operationally safe. The atomic energy industry, however, pursued a different path: "engineered" or "add-on" safety. Under this approach, the underlying technology—the nuclear reactors—may not be completely safe, but nuclear facilities feature add-on elements, such as containers, to guard against the consequences of accidents.

In their book *The Demise of Nuclear Energy? Lessons for Democratic Control of Technology*, Joseph Morone and Edward Woodhouse argue that the path the field of atomic energy took—going with add-ons, rather than inherent safety—probably occurred because decision makers at the time were focused on other issues, mainly timeliness. The decision makers were also operating under the assumption that nuclear power plants would be fairly small—producing about one hundred megawatts each. As the potential of atomic energy was realized, however, plants were ordered at ten times that size. Morone and Woodhouse, and many other atomic energy experts, believe this extraordinary faith in the potential, without full examination of the safety consequences, was short-sighted.

Nevertheless, that path was taken, and the question of whether atomic energy is safe remains an important one. Certainly if one compares the death toll from nuclear power plant accidents in the United States (zero) to the number of deaths that can be attributed to health effects due to air pollution and other environmental effects mentioned above for coal power (unknown, but generally thought to be in the many thousands per year), the answer is clear. Atomic energy, so far, has a better safety record than coal power.

However, the fact that there have been no accidents in the last twenty-five years does not necessarily mean that atomic energy is safe. Interest groups such as the Union of Concerned Scientists remain skeptical. The potential release of radioactive material from a nuclear power plant accident, they say, could kill thousands and leave surrounding land areas unusable for centuries. Even if the risk is small, they argue, the consequences are severe, and risks can stem from so many unknown sources, including and especially the possibility of human error. A former member of the Nuclear Regulatory Commission (N.R.C.) warned, "The abiding lesson that Three Mile Island taught . . . was that a group of N.R.C.-licensed reactor operators, as good as any others, could turn a $2 billion asset into a $1 billion clean up job in about 90 minutes."[5]

The problem of radioactivity is actually a triple threat for atomic energy and its producers. As has already been discussed, it underlies the problem of permanently storing nuclear waste. It underlies the problem of nuclear power plant safety. It also underlies a problem that, particularly since September 11, 2001, has emerged as a new source of public concern: terrorism.

## Terrorism and Nuclear Power Plants

As *Newsweek* reported less than a month after terrorists guided airplanes into New York's World Trade Center, "The consequence of an aircraft's slamming into a nuclear reactor would not be a nuclear explosion. It is physically impossible for the uranium used in U.S. power plants, which typically is less than 5 percent pure, to be fashioned into a Hiroshima-type bomb. . . . The real danger of a terror attack is the release of radioactive contaminants."[6]

The consensus among terrorism experts seems to be that nuclear power plants could be vulnerable either as targets of airplane attacks or from potential terrorists obtaining entrance to a facility under false pretenses (getting jobs as nuclear operators, for example). In the case of an airplane attack, the idea is to crash into the facility, causing a breach that releases radioactive material into the air, or to crash into a holding pool containing radioactive material, displacing and pushing the material out into the air. Otherwise, should a potential terrorist gain entrance to a facility, he or she could presumably incite a meltdown by tampering with the controls.

It is hard to say how likely either of these scenarios is, especially in light of the many choices terrorist have for potential targets in the United States and abroad—all types of public buildings, facilities, and infrastructures, including bridges, mass transit, and stadiums, to name a few. Public fear, however, is undeniable.

One other security concern comes from the possibility of terrorists or unfriendly governments obtaining nuclear weapons capabilities due in part to U.S. assistance in pursuing peaceful atomic energy. A by-product of atomic energy production is plutonium, a crucial ingredient in making an atomic bomb. The United States and several other countries have atomic bomb capabilities. Many countries and terrorist organizations would like to have them. Concern that pursuing atomic energy could potentially pass on this capability has precedence. As Catherine Auer of the *Bulletin of the Atomic Scientists* relates, "India . . . promised to keep its atomic activities peaceful, and on the basis of its assurances, in 1955 Canada built it a research reactor, and the United States supplied heavy water. Thanks to these . . . contributions, India was able to derive approximately 600 pounds of plutonium, some of which it used in a 1974 nuclear [bomb] test."[7] India is now one of a handful of countries with nuclear weapons capabilities. In the same article, Auer notes: "Iran, which has, among other things, a U.S.-supplied research reactor, as well as a power plant being built with foreign assistance, says it has only peaceful purposes in mind for its growing nuclear energy complex. Intelligence organizations believe otherwise."[8]

Radioactivity is a problem that will not go away for the atomic energy industry. The United States does not have an operating permanent storage facility for radioactive waste, and interest groups and the public still fear the possibility of a reactor accident that would disperse radioactive material into the environment. They now also fear the possibility of a terrorist attack on a nuclear power plant. Even if the engineering and economics ultimately work out so that atomic energy becomes "too cheap to meter," it is not clear that it can ever overcome its threefold problem with radioactivity.

With all these concerns, many scientists and energy officials agree that atomic energy does not appear to have anything specific going for it. Despite early expectations, it has not become the cheapest energy option. It is not the cleanest (due to radioactive waste), and it is not the safest—at least not in the public perception. To many, atomic energy has not lived up to expectations. Whether it is likely to disappear as an energy source in the United States within the century will depend greatly on how and if these perceptions and problems can be overcome.

## Notes

1. Dashka Slater, "Free-Market Fallout," *Sierra*, September 2001, p. 14.
2. Quoted in Matthew L. Wald, "Interest in Building Reactors, but Industry Is Still Cautious," *New York Times*, May 2, 2005, p. 19A.
3. Amory B. Lovins and L. Hunter Lovins, "Opposing View: It's Too Costly and Too Risky. More Energy-Efficient Alternatives Exist," *USA Today*, April 17, 2001, p. 12A.
4. Edward Teller, letter to Sterling Cole, chairman, Joint Committee on Atomic Energy, July 23, 1953.
5. Quoted in Wald, "Interest in Building Reactors," p. 19A.
6. *Newsweek*, "Nuclear Power Plants," November 5, 2001, p. 32.
7. Catherine Auer, "Atoms for What?" *Bulletin of the Atomic Scientists*, November/December, 2003, p. 43.
8. Auer, "Atoms for What?" p. 43.

**CHAPTER 1**

# Finding Energy in the Atom

# Discovering Radioactivity

## By Henry N. Wagner Jr. and Linda E. Ketchum

Uranium, an element with ninety-two protons in its nucleus, is the heaviest element found in nature. It is also radioactive, a property discovered by French physicist Henri Becquerel at the end of the nineteenth century. Radioactivity is the spontaneous emission of energy from an atom. Working off the discovery of X-rays by German physicist Wilhelm Conrad Roentgen, Becquerel found that uranium emitted energy rays even after sitting in the dark for more than a year.

The following selection by Henry N. Wagner Jr. and Linda E. Ketchum, a professor of public health and a medical editor, respectively, describes Becquerel's work as well as the subsequent discoveries made by French physicists Marie Curie (born Marya Sklodowska in Poland) and her husband Pierre Curie. The Curies devoted their lives to the study of radioactivity, discovering two new radioactive elements. Though Pierre Curie died in 1906 in an unfortunate accident, Marie Curie went on to win two Nobel prizes for her work. She died in 1934 of radiation poisoning from years of working with radioactive elements.

In 1669, while searching for the "philosopher's stone" to change baser metals into gold, the alchemist Hennig Brand discovered phosphorus. By the mid 1770s, about twenty other elements had been discovered. By 1800, a rash of new elements, including uranium and thorium, had been found. Uranium possesses qualities beyond the wildest dreams of seventeenth-century alchemists. Few people realize that it is more abundant in the earth's crust than the elements cadmium, bismuth, mercury, silver, or iodine.

Henry N. Wagner Jr. and Linda E. Ketchum, *Living with Radiation: The Risk, the Promise*. Baltimore: The Johns Hopkins University Press, 1989. Copyright © 1989 by The Johns Hopkins University Press. All rights reserved. Reproduced by permission.

# Discovering Radioactivity

Potassium uranyl sulfate, a uranium salt, attracted the interest of physicist Henri Becquerel, a professor at the Museum of Natural History in Paris, because it was fluorescent, emitting visible light after exposure to sunlight. The year was 1895, and physicists throughout the world were excited by the German physicist Wilhelm Conrad Roentgen's discovery of "a new kind of ray," a ray with a penetrating power so great that it could go through the human body and reveal broken bones or foreign objects such as bullets. Within a year of the announcement of Roentgen's discovery, more than one thousand publications about X-rays had appeared.

The rays that Roentgen observed originated at the fluorescent spot where an electron beam struck a metal target. Becquerel had an idea that X-rays and visible fluorescent light might be produced by the same mechanism. He was wrong, but, as often happens in scientific research, the wrong hypothesis led to one of the most important discoveries of all time—the discovery of radioactivity.

Becquerel exposed crystals of potassium uranyl sulfate to sunlight to make them fluoresce. His procedure consisted of exposing a piece of ore to sunlight, laying it on photographic film, and wrapping both in dark paper to record any fluorescence that might have been produced. One day, he happened to develop a film that had been exposed to uranium ore that he had never exposed to sunlight. To his surprise, the film was darkened under the piece of ore even though the sun could not possibly have produced fluorescence. Becquerel's observation, remarkable in its simplicity but momentous in its significance, is a classic example of serendipity, an important discovery made by accident. His simple experiments opened up the new science of radioactivity, and eventually led to an understanding of the internal structure of matter and of the interchangeability of matter and energy.

Becquerel discovered that, like X-rays, the mysterious rays from uranium discharged the electric charge on an instrument called a gold-leaf electroscope. This made it possible to measure the rays, which was essential for further scientific investigation. Like Roentgen's rays, Becquerel's rays were "ionizing radiation"—that is, they were capable of producing ions in air. When Becquerel examined other uranium salts and fluorescent compounds of calcium and zinc with his electroscope, he found that even nonfluorescent uranium compounds produced the rays, while fluorescent copper and zinc did not. The one constant factor in all of his experiments was not fluorescence but uranium itself. Could the element uranium be producing the rays?

Becquerel asked a friend, Henri Moissan, to prepare a disk of pure metallic uranium. He then found that pure metal discharged his gold-leaf electroscope with four times the intensity of the uranium ore. Becquerel had no idea what caused the rays or how they could possibly continue to be emitted even after the uranium had remained in darkness for as long as a year, but he realized the great significance of his discovery. Nevertheless, in 1897 he put aside his uranium investigations and returned to his original preoccupation with fluorescence and optics. It remained for one of the most remarkable women of all time to bring about the nuclear age.

## A Woman with a Dream

Marya Sklodowska had the characteristics of many creative scientists: dissatisfaction with the status quo, overwhelming curiosity about nature, limitless energy and endurance, and great intelligence. As a teenager, she dreamed that one day she would give up her job caring for the two children of wealthy Polish lawyers and become a scientist. Every day she found time to study physics, anatomy, physiology, and sociology, and one day she received a letter from her older sister, Bronya, inviting her to come to Paris and study at the Sorbonne.

On November 3, 1891, she began classes in the Faculty of Science, registering as "Marie Sklodowska," thus beginning her adaptation to life in France, where she would spend the rest of her days. All of Marie's time and energy were consumed by lectures and study, and after three years she desperately wanted a laboratory in which to carry out her own experiments. A visiting Polish physics professor suggested that she approach the physicist Pierre Curie to try to find a suitable laboratory. Thirty-five-year-old Pierre was attracted by the ascetic young Polish student, and their friendship grew over the next few months. Pierre began to question his resolve never to marry as Marie's intelligence, dedication, and character made him think that love might, after all, be compatible with his life as a scientist. According to their daughter Ève, Pierre vowed to "win the girl, the Pole, and the physicist, three persons who have become indispensable to me." At first, Marie was not enthusiastic about the idea of marrying a Frenchman, leaving her family, and abandoning her beloved Poland, but she finally decided that "we cannot endure the idea of separating," and Marie and Pierre were married on July 26, 1895. Marya Sklodowska became Madame Curie, a woman who was to achieve world-wide fame.

In 1897, searching for a suitable research subject for her doctoral thesis, Marie came across Becquerel's paper describing the new, mysterious rays. What could be causing them? Where could the energy be coming from? The continual emission of energy rays violated all known principles of physics. If she could answer these questions, certainly she would be awarded the sought-after doctoral degree. But what if she couldn't? Should she choose a "safer" subject for her research? Wasn't it too risky to try to solve such a mystery? Her choice of the courageous path rather than the safe and secure one made all the difference.

## A New Radioactive Element

Marie's first step in the study of the rays of uranium was to learn how to measure them. Instead of using the gold-leaf electroscope, Becquerel's instrument, she turned to an invention by her husband, Pierre, and his brother, Jacques: a new pressure-sensitive crystal that generated electricity when exposed to the uranium rays. With this device, Marie discovered, as had Becquerel, that the intensity of the emitted radiation was proportional to the amount of uranium in the samples. The radiation was not affected by the chemical state of the uranium or by physical factors such as heat or light. To find out whether compounds other than uranium emitted similar rays, Marie examined every element she could get her hands on, and found only one other element that did, thorium.

"We shall call the mysterious rays 'radioactivity,'" she told Pierre, and the substances that produce the rays "radioelements." As she examined one mineral sample after another, Marie observed that the "radioactive" rays released from some samples were stronger than could be accounted for by the amount of uranium or thorium they contained. They seemed to contain a much more powerful radioactive substance than either uranium or thorium. After she had examined all known elements for radioactivity, she became convinced that she must be dealing with a new element, a radioactive element. She told her sister Bronya, "The element is there. I've got to find it. We are sure! The physicists we have spoken to believe we have made an error in experiment and advise us to be careful. But I am convinced that I am not mistaken."

By April 12, 1898, Marie had enough data to announce the probable presence in pitchblende ores of a new element that emitted radiation. Proving its existence was to require superhuman efforts by both Marie and Pierre, who had abandoned his study of crystals to help Marie in her damp little workroom on the Rue Lhomond in Paris. The Curies found that, even in its crude state, pitchblende contained four times more radioactivity than did uranium, yet it was clear that the new element must be present in extremely small quantities, since it could not be detected by the standard chemical analyses. As it turned out, the unknown element made up only one-millionth of the weight of the pitchblende. Its existence was revealed only by the emitted rays. Marie was able to find the new element by chemically separating fractions of pitchblende, measuring the radioactivity of each separated fraction, and retaining those with the highest amounts of radioactivity. Soon they faced another shock: the radioactivity was concentrated in not one but two chemical fractions. By July 1898, Marie and Pierre were sure of the existence of one of the elements. "Could we call it 'polonium' in honor of Poland?" Marie asked Pierre.

In the *Proceedings* of the French Academy for July 1898, the Curies wrote: "We believe the substance we have extracted from pitchblende contains a metal not yet observed, related to bismuth by its analytical properties. If the existence of this new metal is confirmed, we propose to call it polonium, from the name of the original country of one of us."

## Discovering Radium

A second element, which they called "radium," was announced on December 26, 1898. Proving the existence of the two new elements to the satisfaction of the scientific world would require four more years of intensive work. It was necessary to purify huge quantities of pitchblende in order to obtain pure radium and polonium. The extraction process began with ore obtained from the St. Joachimsthal mines, in Bohemia, mines that were later discovered to be the cause of lung cancer in many of the miners. The cost of the ore itself was far beyond Marie and Pierre's means, so they decided to start with the residue that remained at the mine after the initial extraction to purify the pitchblende. Tons of pitchblende residue in sacks were unloaded on the Rue Lhomond, and they began the separation process in an abandoned shed with a leaky skylight across from the little workshop in the School of Physics. "The shed was so untempting, so miserable that nobody thought of refusing them the use of it," wrote Ève Curie.

Marie later wrote: "And yet it was in this miserable old shed that the best and happiest years of our life were spent, entirely consecrated to work. I sometimes passed the whole day stirring a mass ebullition [boiling substance] with an iron rod nearly as big as myself. In the evening I was broken with fatigue."

The Curies' report in 1900 at the Congress for Physics in Paris stimulated great excitement. It was not long before André Debierne, working in a separate laboratory at the Sorbonne but in constant communication with the Curies, discovered a third new radioelement, named "actinium." In 1902 the Curies announced that they had isolated one-tenth of a gram of pure radium and determined its atomic weight to be 225. Radium officially existed; it was spontaneously luminous, glowed with a bluish phosphorescence, and was two million times more radioactive than uranium. The next major discovery was that radium continuously releases a gas, helium. This was the first known example of one element changing into another, a process called transmutation.

## A New Brand of Science

Radium defied all the current theories concerning the conservation of energy because it continuously radiated heat. Another discovery was that radioactive elements lose half of their radioactivity over a specific period of time. For each radioelement, it takes a characteristic amount of time for the radioactivity to decrease by one-half, called the "half-life," and for each particular radioactive element, that period of time is always the same. For example, it takes several billion years for the radioactivity of uranium to diminish by one-half. The half-life of radium is 1,600 years. Radon, another product of uranium, has a half-life of four days, and the "descendants" or "daughters" of radon have half-lives in seconds. Without Pierre and Marie Curie, uranium might have remained a simple laboratory curiosity, and the new elements might have remained stored in laboratory collections. The Curies' intense efforts and subsequent discoveries gave birth to the radiation sciences. "Philosophers had to begin their philosophy all over again and physicists their physics," wrote Ève Curie.

The finding that an atom's disintegration is entirely independent of environmental and physical conditions left all prior scientific and philosophical theories hanging in midair. The atom—thought to be the most basic physical structure in the universe—not only was able to collapse spontaneously but also did so at frequent intervals, the process of disintegration being governed only by statistical laws.

# Einstein's Theory Reveals How to Get Energy from Atoms

**By William L. Laurence**

Protons and neutrons are bound together within the nucleus of an atom by an extremely powerful force. That force is so powerful that even a small change in the content of the nucleus unleashes a tremendous amount of energy.

The author of the following article, William L. Laurence, was a Pulitzer Prize–winning reporter for the *New York Times* who chronicled the development of atomic energy and the atomic bomb in the 1940s. In this selection, originally published in 1946, he explains that physicist Albert Einstein was the first to understand the theoretical relationship between matter and energy. Einstein's famous equation $E = mc^2$ shows that a very small amount of mass (m) can, in theory, be converted to an amount of energy (E) that is proportional to the squared value of the speed of light (c). This theory served as the foundation for the harnessing and exploitation of atomic energy. Einstein was born in Germany in 1879, converted to Swiss citizenship in early adulthood, and became an American citizen in 1940.

**A**tomic energy, harnessed for the first time by our [American] scientists for use in atomic bombs, is the practically inexhaustible source of power that enables our sun to supply us with heat, light, and other forms of radiant energy, without which life on earth would not be possible. It is the same energy,

William L. Laurence, *Dawn over Zero: The Story of the Atomic Bomb*. Westport, CT: Greenwood Press, 1972.

stored in the nuclei of the atoms of the material universe, that keeps the stars, bodies much larger than our sun, radiating their enormous quantities of light and heat for billions of years instead of burning themselves out in periods measured only in thousands of years.

## A Theoretical Discovery

The existence of atomic energy was first discovered by Einstein about forty years ago on purely theoretical grounds, as an outgrowth of his famous theory of relativity, according to which a body in motion has a greater mass than the same body at rest, this increase in mass bearing a direct relationship to the velocity of light. This meant that the energy of motion imparts an actual increase in mass.

From the formula for the relationship of this increase of mass to the velocity of light Einstein derived his famous mathematical equation that revealed for the first time an equivalence between mass and energy, one of the most revolutionary concepts in the intellectual history of mankind. The mass-energy equation showed that any given quantity of mass is the equivalent of a specific amount of energy, and vice versa.

Specifically this equation revealed the fact, incredible at that time, that very small amounts of matter contain tremendous amounts of energy. A piece of coal the size of a pea, the equation proved, contains enough energy to drive the largest ocean liner across the Atlantic and back. No one, however, least of all Einstein himself, believed at that time that any means could ever be found to tap this cosmic source of elemental energy.

## Einstein's Formula: $E = mc^2$

In the mass-energy theorem Einstein showed the existence of a definite relationship between the cosmic trinity of matter, energy, and the velocity of light. The relationship is so simple that, once arrived at, a grammar-school student could work it out. In this formula the letter $m$ stands for mass in terms of grams; the letter $E$ represents energy in terms of ergs (a small unit of energy or work); the letter $c$ stands for the velocity of light in terms of centimeters per second. The energy content of any given quantity of any substance, the formula states, is equal to the mass of the substance (in terms of grams) multiplied by the square of the velocity of light (in terms of centimeters per second). The velocity of light (in round numbers) is 300,000 kilometers, or 30,000,000,000 centimeters, per second.

Take one gram of any substance. According to the Einstein formula, the amount of energy ($E$) in ergs in this mass is equal to 1 (the mass of the substance in grams) multiplied by 30,000,000,000 squared. In other words, the energy content of one gram of matter equals 900 billion billion ergs. Translated into terms of pounds and kilowatt-hours, this means that one pound of matter contains the energy equivalent of 10,000,000,000 kilowatt-hours.

If this energy could be fully utilized, it would take only twenty-two pounds of matter to supply all the electrical power requirements of the United States for a year. One third of a gram of water would yield enough heat to turn 12,000 tons of water into steam. One gram of water would raise a load of a million tons to the top of a mountain six miles high. A breath of air would operate a powerful airplane continuously for a year. A handful of snow would heat a large apartment house for a year. The pasteboard in a small railroad ticket would run a heavy passenger train several times around the world. A cup of water would supply the power of a great generating station of 100,000-kilowatt capacity for six years.

One pound of any substance, if its atomic-energy content could be utilized one hundred per cent, is equivalent in power content to 3,000,000,000 pounds of coal, or 1,500,000 tons. The energy we are now able to utilize in the atomic bombs, at maximum efficiency, constitutes only one tenth of one per cent of the total energy present in the material. But even one hundredth of one per cent would still be by far the most destructive force on this earth.

## A New Type of Energy

Atomic energy, released through the splitting of atoms, differs radically from ordinary types of energy hitherto available to man in that it involves a fundamental change in the nature of the atom, a change in which an appreciable amount of matter is converted into energy.

This is materially different from obtaining power by the use of a water wheel, for example, or by the burning of coal or oil. In the case of the water wheel, the water molecules taking part remain entirely unchanged. They simply lose potential energy as they pass from the dam to the tailrace. In the case of burning coal or oil a more intense process takes place, as the atoms of carbon, hydrogen, and oxygen (of which the coal and oil molecules are composed) are regrouped by combustion into new molecules forming new substances. The atoms themselves, however, still remain unchanged—they still are carbon, hydrogen, and oxygen. None of them, so far as can be measured, loses any part of its mass.

In the case of atomic energy, however, the atom itself completely changes its identity, and in this process of change it loses part of its mass, which is converted into energy. The amount of energy liberated in this process is directly proportional to the amount of atomic mass destroyed.

## Atomic Energy from the Sun

The sun, for example, obtains its energy through the partial destruction of its hydrogen, through a complex process in which the hydrogen is converted into helium. In this process four hydrogen atoms, each with an atomic mass of 1.008 (total, 4.032 atomic mass units) combine to form one helium atom, which has an atomic mass of 4.003. This represents a loss of mass in the four hydrogen atoms (in addition to a loss of two positive electrons) of 0.029 atomic mass units, which is coverted into pure energy. The amount of energy liberated in this process by the enormous quantities of hydrogen in the sun represents an actual loss of the sun's mass at the rate of 4,000,000 tons per second, a mere speck of dust in relation to the sun's total mass of two billion billion billion tons.

If the sun, however, were a mass of coal weighing the same amount, it would have to burn three billion times the mass it is burning now to produce the same amount of energy. If that were the case, it would have used up the entire store of molecular energy contained in its body of coal in the course of 5,750 years. In other words, it would have burned out long before the earth was born.

By the use of atomic energy the sun has been able to give off its enormous amounts of radiation for a period estimated at 10 billion years, and its mass, at the present rate of burning, is enough to last 15,000 billion years more, although, of course, the amount of its radiation would be greatly reduced long before that in proportion to the decrease of its mass. Radiations in amounts sufficient to support life on earth are estimated to continue for some ten billion to a hundred billion years longer.

# An Amazing Array of Nuclear Discoveries in the 1930s

## By Richard L. Garwin and Georges Charpak

The 1930s were literally an explosive decade for nuclear research. In 1932 British physicist James Chadwick discovered the neutron, which furnished physicists with the particle they needed to generate nuclear reactions. Within a few years, physicists were producing fission, though they did not recognize the concept as such until 1939 when Austrian physicist Lise Meitner, in exile in Sweden, and her nephew Otto Frisch coined the term in an article published in the scientific journal *Nature*. In less than ten years, physicists had laid the groundwork for the production of nuclear chain reactions.

In this selection, Richard L. Garwin, an Enrico Fermi award winner, and Georges Charpak, a Nobel Prize laureate in physics, describe this amazing decade, as well as the early years of World War II when the science of atomic energy was developed for practical and deadly use.

U ntil 1945, nuclear energy manifested itself either on a very large scale appropriate to the evolution of the universe, in the sun and the other stars, or on the microscopic scale of reactions that could be produced in the laboratory between isolated nuclei. Many, even among the greatest physicists, believed that it would never be possible to tap this immense reserve of energy contained in the mass of atomic nuclei. [Albert] Einstein once said that it was as likely as a blind man hunting a bird in a country where there were very few birds. Nuclear physics was long considered simply a fundamental science without any prospect of serious application. But as sometimes happens in science, a basic discovery, by researchers who had no inkling of the consequences, turned everything topsy-turvy. The fate of our civilization was suddenly put at risk.

## Discovering the Neutron

In 1932, the British physicist James Chadwick discovered the neutron, emitted when beryllium was bombarded with alpha particles from radioactive materials. He proposed that the alpha particle combines with the beryllium nucleus of 9 atomic mass units to form carbon with 12 atomic mass units, plus a free neutron. The term "neutron" had been applied long before its discovery to a hypothetical particle that would solve some of the paradoxes inherent in imagining nuclei to be made up of protons and of nuclear electrons that compensated the charge of about half of the protons. Chadwick himself thought he had discovered a proton-electron compound much smaller than the hydrogen atom. It took a little while before he and other physicists became convinced that what he had actually found was a new fundamental particle that accounts for more than half of the mass of the objects around us. With the neutron one had a projectile to induce nuclear reactions which, in contrast to the proton, was not inhibited by the electric charge of the nucleus. A proton approaching a nucleus is repelled by the positive charge of the nuclear protons; with neutrons it is possible to penetrate heavy nuclei which, like uranium, contain many protons (uranium has 92) and hence strongly repel positively charged projectiles such as protons.

## The Neutron as a Projectile

Alchemists had tried for centuries to transmute lead into gold, but by Chadwick's time it was well understood that the nucleus was unaffected by chemical manipulations. Up to that time the projectiles that had been used to probe the interiors of atoms were positively charged protons, or alpha particles emitted by radioactive sources. Before the First World War, Pierre and Marie Curie were pioneers in the fabrication of powerful radioactive sources. (Their long-term exposure to intense radioactivity eventually ruined the health of both.) In the infant science of nuclear physics, these sources played the role that particle accelerators were later to play. Their use led to many fundamental discoveries, in particular to the discovery of "artificial radioactivity" by Irène [daughter of Marie and Pierre and her husband] Frédéric Joliot-Curie in 1934: radioactive substances are produced when one bombards a normally nonradioactive (stable) element with a nuclear projectile (in their case, boron with alpha particles). These sources were soon replaced by protons brought to high speeds in the cyclotron, a particle accelerator invented and built at Berkeley, California, by the American physicist Ernest O. Lawrence in 1932 (Leo Szilard, who appears later in this saga, independently invented the cyclotron). Following the discovery of artificial radioactivity, [Italian physicist] Enrico Fermi in Rome had the idea of using neutrons as electrically neutral projectiles to achieve nuclear transmutations, that is, the transmutation of the atomic nuclei of one element into those of another.

Although great energy is required for charged particles to penetrate the electrical barrier that surrounds a nucleus, neutrons can slip into a nucleus while being practically at rest. In March 1934, Fermi submitted a paper demonstrating the production of artificial radioactivity by neutron bombardment of aluminum and of fluorine. By December 1934, Fermi had discovered that neutrons whose energy had been dissipated by collisions in paraffin were much more effective than neutrons that had not been slowed down. This was an unexpected result, explainable only by quantum mechanics; naively one might have thought that more energetic neutrons would be more efficient at producing nuclear reactions. Despite the fact that the neutron sources available at the time were extraordinarily weak, the use of slow neutrons opened the door to a flood of discoveries.

## Working with Uranium

Physicists were particularly tempted to irradiate uranium, because it was the heaviest element known to exist in nature: its nucleus contains . . . 92 protons. If a neutron was captured and added to the already existing stock of neutrons, it could create an unstable nucleus that might disintegrate by emitting an electron, so that the nuclear charge would increase by a unit as a neutron transformed itself into a proton plus an electron.

In this process, it turned out that another particle was also emitted, called the neutrino, which has no electrical charge, has a mass small even compared with the mass of an electron, can cross the entire earth without interacting, and is therefore difficult to detect. But it has been detected, and even before it was actually observed, its existence was postulated to maintain the conservation of energy and momentum in these decays.

The capture of a neutron is an inexpensive way to add a proton to a nucleus and thus to produce atoms that are not found in nature because they are unstable. Normally, however, the result of such transmutation is an element of familiar chemistry, since it will have the same number of protons (hence will bind the same number of electrons) as the next higher element in the periodic table. In the case of uranium, there was no known chemical element with one more (a 93rd) proton. Uranium would then have to be transmuted into a completely novel chemical element. By June 1934, Fermi's group in Rome published the results of experiments using neutrons to produce many new types of artificially radioactive material. Among these, the team provided evidence for the creation of a new element, which they ultimately called "ausonium," one whose nucleus was supposed to contain 93 protons, one more than uranium. Their evidence misled them; they had not discovered element 93, but something much more important. The actual discovery of element 93 did not take place until 1940, when Edwin M. McMillan and Philip H. Abelson at Berkeley created and named "neptunium," with a mass number of 239, the result of the decay of uranium-239, whose half-life is 23 minutes. Neptunium-239 decays with a half-life of 2.3 days to plutonium-239; plutonium is element 94.

## A Scientific Detective Story

Over the years 1934 to 1938, the best German, French, and Italian teams attempted to clarify the nature of the radioactive entities produced from uranium by the capture of neutrons. No one, however, thought of the idea of fission—that is, the splitting of a heavy nucleus into two lighter ones, in contrast to the shedding of one or two protons or neutrons. It seemed most plausible that capturing a neutron would simply cause a relatively minor adjustment of the nucleus. But when, at the end of 1938, fission was at last discovered and identified, it was soon realized that it had the potential to revolutionize warfare and could determine the balance of power among nations.

This had been recognized by a Hungarian physicist, Leo Szilard, who figures importantly in this history as a man of vision, vigor, and influence. Living in London, Szilard had filed a patent on March 12, 1934, on the concept of a nuclear chain reaction in which a neutron bombarding a mass of material (he cited beryllium, uranium, or thorium) would produce two neutrons of high energy, which would in turn produce 4, which would produce 8, which would produce sixteen, and so on. Szilard at this point had no clear idea of transmutation caused by neutrons and certainly none of fission. He was later to play a key role in the United States in realizing the first nuclear chain reaction.

The recognition of fission itself is a scientific detective story. In his Nobel Prize acceptance speech in Stockholm on December 10, 1938, Enrico Fermi related that the neutron bombardment of uranium led to one or more elements of atomic number larger than 92 and specifically mentioned elements 93 and 94, now called neptunium and plutonium. His prize was awarded "for his demonstration of the existence of new radioactive elements produced by neutron irradiation, and for his related discovery of nuclear reactions brought about by slow neutrons." He had no idea that his group in Rome had produced fission in uranium for the preceding four years; they did not detect the fission products as they were emitted, because a thin aluminum foil that was intended to shield the detector from the alpha particles from uranium stopped the fission fragments from entering the detector. They had also produced elements 93 and 94, but their experiment provided evidence for the fission products and not for elements of higher atomic number.

## Fission: The Liquid Drop Model

Within a month, Otto Hahn and Fritz Strassmann in Berlin published their work of 1938 identifying some of the products of neutron bombardment of uranium as the element barium, which has 56 protons. As chemists, they were sure of their results; as "nuclear chemists," they were reluctant to bring themselves, as they wrote, "to take such a drastic step which goes against all previous experience in nuclear physics." They could not conceive of a physical mechanism that would burst a uranium nucleus to yield two of about half its mass.

At Christmas 1938, Lise Meitner—a colleague of Hahn and Strassmann's who as a Jew had been forced into exile in Sweden—and her nephew Otto Frisch first thought through the implications of the barium discovery and explained it by applying the "liquid drop" model of the nucleus that had just been invented by [Danish physicist] Niels Bohr; they published their work in *Nature* on February 6, 1939. Capture of a neutron by a uranium nucleus would set the liquid drop into oscillation violent enough so that it would split in two. Frisch termed the process "fission" by analogy to the division of biological cells. The fission products, made up of lighter nuclei, were created with considerable kinetic energy whose value, expressed in mass units, represented about a thousandth of the initial mass of the uranium nucleus.

In December 1938, Fermi had left Italy with his family to receive the Nobel Prize in Sweden, intending not to return. Arriving in New York on January 2, 1939, he was welcomed to the physics department at Columbia University. Two weeks later, Fermi and his wife, Laura, greeted Bohr as he came from Denmark with the as-yet-unpublished news that Meitner and Frisch had confirmed the process of nuclear fission by "radiochemical" experiments (i.e., using chemistry to characterize the radioactive materials resulting from neutron-induced fission of uranium). Fermi was interested in fission as a new physical phenomenon, but Szilard, who had moved to New York in November 1938, saw in fission the near certainty of nuclear explosives—the realization of his five-year fixation on the chain reaction. In 1932, Szilard had read the H.G. Wells novel *The World Set Free*, published in 1914, in which the major cities of the world are destroyed by atomic bombs in 1956.

On February 19, 1939, Frisch (in Copenhagen) published an experimental verification of the Hahn-Strassmann results by observing large signals from fission fragments in an ionization chamber. The ionization chamber is a basic tool of physics used at that time to detect alpha particles. After being emitted by a nucleus, such a particle travels a few centimeters in air, losing its energy by stripping electrons from hundreds of thousands of atoms. A sensitive electronic amplifier detects the electric charge from all these ions drawn to a negative electrode (or the electrons drawn to a positive metal plate). Comparison with the signal from a typical 6 MeV (million-electron-volt) alpha particle made it clear that the fission process liberated nearly 200 MeV.

# A Special Isotope: U-235

In February 1939, at Princeton, Bohr conjectured that fission by slow neutrons occurs in one special isotope [the same element with different number of neutrons] of uranium—uranium-235. That month, using the liquid-drop model, Bohr and John Wheeler calculated neutron energies required to induce fission. A neutron captured by a heavy nucleus provokes the nucleus to vibrate an energy equal to the neutron binding energy plus any kinetic energy the neutron may have had; with sufficiently large neutron energy, the excited nucleus rapidly splits apart, while for lesser neutron energies the excitation is eventually emitted as gamma rays. They found that a neutron energy of 0.6 MeV would be needed to cause fission in uranium-238 and about zero for uranium-235 (slightly negative—i.e., the energy given to the uranium-235 nucleus by the 8-MeV binding energy of an additional neutron is above the threshold for fission, without the need for any kinetic energy of the neutron), thus confirming Bohr's conjecture that fission by slow neutrons in natural uranium was due to the rare (0.71% abundant) uranium-235. This theoretical prediction was proved in March by Alfred O. Nier and his colleagues in Minnesota. They observed a higher fission yield from a sample of uranium that they had managed to enrich in uranium-235 content.

In 1939, more than a hundred articles devoted to fission were published in scientific journals. Work had begun in the United States, Germany, and Japan, among other countries. In France, Frédéric Joliot (who had married Irène Curie and taken the name Joliot-Curie) and his collaborators had applied for a patent on a "device for producing energy" and "improvements to explosive charges." Of utmost importance, the fission was accompanied by the emission of several neutrons—a possibility mentioned by Fermi in a January 1939 speech in Washington and established by March 1939. In April 1939, Frédéric Joliot-Curie, Lew Kowarski, and Hans von Halban in Paris found an average of 3.5 ± 0.7 neutrons per fission, while Szilard and Walter H. Zinn at Columbia University found about two. For uranium-235 fission by slow neutrons—i.e., neutrons that had only the thermal energy of the environment—the number was later determined more accurately as 2.4. This made a chain reaction possible, a neutron from each fission causing an additional fission. Even in natural uranium, a chain reaction could take place if somehow the large amount of uranium-238 could be prevented from gobbling up too many of

## Uranium-235 Fission Scenario

1. Initial state: the neutron and the uranium-235 nucleus are almost at rest, at room temperature.

2. Intermediate state: the neutron has been incorporated into the nucleus, which vibrates like a drop of water before breaking up. The reader can fill a balloon with water, tap on it, and see how it vibrates.

3. The nuclear "droplet" has split, giving way to two lighter radioactive nuclei whose kinetic energy is 150 MeV, and to two or three neutrons whose energy is 2 MeV each.

The electron volt (eV) corresponds to the energy acquired by an electron accelerated in a vacuum by a potential of one volt, about the voltage of the familiar dry cell. It requires about ten electron volts (10 eV) to extract an electron from an atom, and about ten million electron volts (10 MeV) to extract a neutron or a proton from a nucleus.

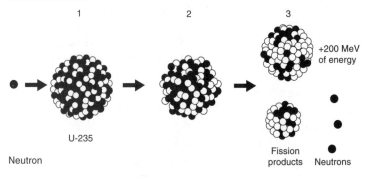

*Fig. 1. Chain reaction scenario.*

The energy of the fission products corresponds to the energy of the atoms in a medium raised to a temperature of many billions of degrees. The sum of the kinetic energies of the two fission-product nuclei is almost equal to the energy $E = Mc^2$, where $M$ is the difference in mass between the initial nucleus and the sum of the final nuclei.

the emitted neutrons; uranium-238 does not fission with slow neutrons and has only about one-fifth the probability of fission with fast neutrons that uranium-235 has. The chain reaction, if it can be achieved, allows the passage from the infinitesimally small individual nuclear reaction to a reaction involving millions of billions of billions of nuclei.

Such a chain reaction using neutrons of fission energy is equivalent to compound interest that doubles capital every hundred-millionth of a second. It was evident to the physicists of the day that if one could produce fission on a large scale, an energy equivalent to that from the explosion of a ton of a powerful explosive like TNT could be extracted from sixty thousandths of a gram (60 milligrams) of uranium. It follows from Frisch's discovery that uranium fission liberates as energy about a thousandth of the mass of the material: from 60 milligrams of uranium could be obtained 60 micrograms of energy, and $E = Mc^2$ gives us $6 \times 10^{-8} \times 9 \times 10^{16}$ $= 5.4 \times 10^9$ joules. The energy release of one gram of high explosive is about one thousand calories or 4186 joules, so that one ton of high explosive is just about $4.2 \times 10^9$ joules.

At Columbia, as in laboratories the world over, physicists scrambled to explore the new phenomenon of fission, while Fermi, with Szilard's urging, worked toward the goal of a self-sustaining fission reaction. In July 1939, Szilard prodded Fermi to start a large-scale experimental pile with "perhaps 50 tons of graphite and 5 tons of uranium," and by November 1, a new "Advisory Committee on Uranium" recommended purchases on that scale.

## Making an Atomic Bomb

The Second World War completely changed the conditions under which work on fission was conducted. At the strong suggestion of Albert Einstein—who had been alerted to the possible uses of fission (and to the fact that the Germans were already working on it) by the Hungarian refugee physicists Eugene Wigner and Leo Szilard—President Franklin Roosevelt decided to launch research to avoid being caught short by the Nazis. His conviction, and that of his scientific advisors, was reinforced by a secret report by the physicists Rudolph E. Peierls and Otto Frisch, two German Jewish emigrants who had taken refuge in Birmingham, England. They calculated that a relatively small amount of uranium-235—something like ten pounds as opposed to tons—would suffice to retain enough of the fission neutrons to cause an expanding number of fissions and so to make a bomb. They communicated this to the British authorities, who in 1941 passed the information on to Washington. Specifically, in July 1941 the "Maud Committee" established by the British government concluded that it would take some three years to make a nuclear weapon and would require a few kilograms of uranium-235.

In the United States, the Manhattan Project, as the nuclear weapons program was called, benefited not only from the excellent community of American physicists and the American capacity for organization and production but also from the help of European physicists who had fled Nazism. With the Japanese attack on Pearl Harbor on December 7, 1941, and the immediate U.S. entry thereupon into the war against Japan and Germany, all scientific and technical resources in the United States were mobilized in the service of the war effort for the duration of the conflict.

Szilard's efforts bore fruit. On December 2, 1942, Fermi put into operation at the University of Chicago the first atomic "pile"—a "nuclear reactor"—using the controlled propagation of fission in uranium-235 in a stack (or pile) of natural uranium lumps (metal and oxide) distributed in a pile of graphite blocks. Although at Columbia Fermi had made experimental piles of graphite and uranium oxide, it was only at Chicago that he had sufficiently pure material and enough of it for a self-sustaining fission reaction.

By the beginning of the Second World War, physicists had concluded that it was possible to exploit the formidable binding energy of atomic nuclei to make either explosives of unequaled power or fuel, a fuel whose mass would be millions of times smaller than that of traditional fuels, whose energy production is based on the interactions between atomic orbital electrons. Fermi had the good fortune to be able to accomplish this work in the United States, far from the ravages of war and, above all, with the immense resources that the United States would then contribute to drive the Nazis and the Japanese from conquered territories.

# The First Controlled Chain Reaction

## By Corbin Allardice and Edward R. Trapnell

Italian physicist Enrico Fermi was awarded the Nobel Prize in physics in 1938 for his work with neutrons. Immediately afterward, he emigrated to the United States, escaping Benito Mussolini's fascist regime in Italy.

Fermi's early work led to the 1939 discovery of fission: the splitting of an element such as uranium by bombarding its nucleus with a neutron. The process of fission releases additional neutrons from the nucleus. Fermi figured the released neutrons were free to bombard additional uranium nuclei. This releases yet more neutrons that can bombard even more nuclei, thus generating a sustained set of fission reactions, or a chain reaction.

The following selection describes Fermi's first successful, controlled chain reaction. It took place on a squash court beneath a football field at the University of Chicago. Corbin Allardice and Edward R. Trapnell, the authors of this selection, were public information officers for the Atomic Energy Commission. They wrote this story in 1946 after interviewing dozens of scientists who were present at the experiment.

On December 2, 1942, man first initiated a self-sustaining nuclear chain reaction, and controlled it.

Beneath the West Stands of Stagg Field, Chicago, late in the afternoon of that day, a small group of scientists witnessed the advent of a new era in science. History was made in what had been a squash-rackets court.

Corbin Allardice and Edward R. Trapnell, "The First Pile," *The First Reactor*. Washington, DC: U.S. Department of Energy, December 1982.

Precisely at 3:25 P.M., Chicago time, scientist George Weil withdrew the cadmium-plated control rod and by his action man unleashed and controlled the energy of the atom.

As those who witnessed the experiment became aware of what had happened, smiles spread over their faces and a quiet ripple of applause could be heard. It was a tribute to Enrico Fermi, Nobel Prize winner, to whom, more than to any other person, the success of the experiment was due.

Fermi, born in Rome, Italy, on September 29, 1901, had been working with uranium for many years. In 1934 he bombarded uranium with neutrons and produced what appeared to be element 93 (uranium is element 92) and element 94. However, after closer examination it seemed as if nature had gone wild; several other elements were present, but none could be fitted into the periodic table near uranium—where Fermi knew they should have fitted if they had been the transuranic elements 93 and 94. It was not until five years later that anyone, Fermi included, realized he had actually caused fission of the uranium and that these unexplained elements belonged back in the middle part of the periodic table.

Fermi was awarded the Nobel Prize in 1938 for his work on transuranic elements. He and his family went to Sweden to receive the prize. The Italian Fascist press severely criticized him for not wearing a Fascist uniform and failing to give the Fascist salute when he received the award. The Fermis never returned to Italy.

From Sweden, having taken most of his personal possessions with him, Fermi proceeded to London and thence to America where he has remained ever since.

The modern Italian explorer of the unknown was in Chicago that cold December day in 1942. An outsider looking into the squash court where Fermi was working would have been greeted by a strange sight. In the center of the 30- by 60-foot room, shrouded on all but one side by a gray balloon cloth envelope, was a pile of black bricks and wooden timbers, square at the bottom and a flattened sphere on top. Up to half of its height, its sides were straight. The top half was domed, like a beehive. During the construction of this crude appearing but complex pile (the name which has since been applied to all such devices) the standing joke among the scientists working on it was: "If people could see what we're doing with a million-and-a-half of their dollars, they'd think we are crazy. If they knew why we are doing it, they'd be sure we are."

In relation to the fabulous atomic bomb program, of which the

Chicago Pile experiment was a key part, the successful result reported on December 2nd formed one more piece for the jigsaw puzzle which was atomic energy. Confirmation of the chain reactor studies was an inspiration to the leaders of the bomb project, and reassuring at the same time, because the Army's Manhattan Engineer District had moved ahead on many fronts. Contract negotiations were under way to build production-scale nuclear chain reactors, land had been acquired at Oak Ridge, Tennessee, and millions of dollars had been obligated.

Three years before the December 2nd experiment, it had been discovered that when an atom of uranium was bombarded by neutrons, the uranium atom sometimes was split, or fissioned. Later, it had been found that when an atom of uranium fissioned, additional neutrons were emitted and became available for further reaction with other uranium atoms. These facts implied the possibility of a chain reaction, similar in certain respects to the reaction which is the source of the sun's energy. The facts further indicated that if a sufficient quantity of uranium could be brought together under the proper conditions, a self-sustaining chain reaction would result. This quantity of uranium necessary for a chain reaction under given conditions is known as the critical mass, or more commonly, the "critical size" of the particular pile.

For three years the problem of a self-sustaining chain reaction had been assiduously studied. Nearly a year after Pearl Harbor, a pile of critical size was finally constructed. It worked. A self-sustaining nuclear chain reaction was a reality. . . .

## Construction of the Pile

Construction of the main pile at Chicago started in November. The project gained momentum, with machining of the graphite blocks, pressing of the uranium oxide pellets, and the design of instruments. Fermi's two "construction" crews, one under [Walter H.] Zinn and the other under [Herbert L.] Anderson, worked almost around the clock. V.C. Wilson headed up the instrument work.

Original estimates as to the critical size of the pile were pessimistic. As a further precaution, it was decided to enclose the pile in a balloon cloth bag which could be evacuated to remove the neutron-capturing air.

This balloon cloth bag was constructed by Goodyear Tire and Rubber Company. Specialists in designing gasbags for lighter-than-air craft, the company's engineers were a bit puzzled about the aerodynamics of a square balloon. Security regulations forbade informing Goodyear of the purpose of the envelope and so the Army's new square balloon was the butt of much joking.

The bag was hung with one side left open; in the center of the floor a circular layer of graphite bricks was placed. This and each succeeding layer of the pile was braced by a wooden frame. Alternate layers contained the uranium. By this layer-on-layer construction a roughly spherical pile of uranium and graphite was formed.

Facilities for the machining of graphite bricks were installed in the West Stands. Week after week this shop turned out graphite bricks. This work was done under the direction of Zinn's group, by skilled mechanics led by millwright August Knuth. In October, Anderson and his associates joined Zinn's men.

Describing this phase of the work, Albert Wattenberg, one of Zinn's group, said: "We found out how coal miners feel. After eight hours of machining graphite, we looked as if we were made up for a minstrel [show]. One shower would remove only the surface graphite dust. About a half-hour after the first shower the dust in the pores of your skin would start oozing. Walking around the room where we cut the graphite was like walking on a dance floor. Graphite is a dry lubricant, you know, and the cement floor covered with graphite dust was slippery."

Before the structure was half complete, measurements indicated that the critical size at which the pile would become self-sustaining was somewhat less than had been anticipated in the design.

## Computations Forecast Success

Day after day the pile grew toward its final shape. And as the size of the pile increased, so did the nervous tension of the men working on it. Logically and scientifically they knew this pile would become self-sustaining. It had to. All the measurements indicated that it would. But still the demonstration had to be made. As the eagerly awaited moment drew nearer, the scientists gave greater and greater attention to details, the accuracy of measurements, and exactness of their construction work.

Guiding the entire pile construction and design was the nimble-brained Fermi, whose associates described him as "completely self-confident but wholly without conceit."

So exact were Fermi's calculations, based on the measurements taken from the partially finished pile, that days before its completion and demonstration on December 2nd, he was able to predict almost to the exact brick the point at which the reactor would become self-sustaining.

But with all their care and confidence, few in the group knew the extent of the heavy bets being placed on their success. In Washington, the Manhattan District [the Army project tasked with developing an atomic bomb] had proceeded with negotiations with E.I. duPont de Nemours and Company to design, build, and operate a plant based on the principles of the then unproved Chicago pile. The $350,000,000 Hanford Engineer Works at Pasco, Washington, was to be the result.

At Chicago during the early afternoon of December 1st, tests indicated that critical size was rapidly being approached. At 4:00 P.M. Zinn's group was relieved by the men working under Anderson. Shortly afterwards, the last layer of graphite and uranium bricks was placed on the pile. Zinn, who remained, and Anderson made several measurements of the activity within the pile. They were certain that when the control rods were withdrawn, the pile would become self-sustaining. Both had agreed, however, that should measurements indicate the reaction would become self-sustaining when the rods were withdrawn, they would not start the pile operating until Fermi and the rest of the group could be present. Consequently, the control rods were locked and further work was postponed until the following day.

That night the word was passed to the men who had worked on the pile that the trial run was due the next morning.

## Assembly for the Test

About 8:30 on the morning of Wednesday, December 2nd, the group began to assemble in the squash court.

At the north end of the squash court was a balcony about ten feet above the floor of the court. Fermi, Zinn, Anderson, and [project director Arthur H.] Compton were grouped around instruments at the east end of the balcony. The remainder of the observers crowded the little balcony. R.G. Nobles, one of the young scientists who worked on the pile, put it this way: "The control cabinet was surrounded by the 'big wheels'; the 'little wheels' had to stand back."

On the floor of the squash court, just beneath the balcony, stood George Weil, whose duty it was to handle the final control rods. In the pile were three sets of control rods. One set was automatic and could be controlled from the balcony. Another was an emergency safety rod. Attached to one end of this rod was a rope running through the pile and weighted heavily on the opposite end. The rod was withdrawn from the pile and tied by another rope to the balcony. [Norman] Hilberry was ready to cut this rope with an axe should something unexpected happen, or in case the automatic safety rods failed. The third rod, operated by Weil, was the one which actually held the reaction in check until withdrawn the proper distance.

Since this demonstration was new and different from anything ever done before, complete reliance was not placed on mechanically operated control rods. Therefore, a "liquid-control squad," composed of Harold Lichtenberger, W. Nyer, and A.C. Graves, stood on a platform above the pile. They were prepared to flood the pile with cadmium-salt solution in case of mechanical failure of the control rods.

Each group rehearsed its part of the experiment.

At 9:45 Fermi ordered the electrically operated control rods withdrawn. The man at the controls threw the switch to withdraw them. A small motor whined. All eyes watched the lights which indicated the rods' position.

But quickly, the balcony group turned to watch the counters, whose clicking stepped up after the rods were out. The indicators of these counters resembled the face of a clock, with "hands" to indicate neutron count. Nearby was a recorder, whose quivering pen traced the neutron activity within the pile.

Shortly after ten o'clock, Fermi ordered the emergency rod, called "Zip," pulled out and tied.

"Zip out," said Fermi. Zinn withdrew "Zip" by hand and tied it to the balcony rail. Weil stood ready by the "vernier" control rod which was marked to show the number of feet and inches which remained within the pile.

At 10:37 Fermi, without taking his eyes off the instruments, said quietly:

"Pull it to 13 feet, George." The counters clicked faster. The graph pen moved up. All the instruments were studied, and computations were made.

"This is not it," said Fermi. "The trace will go to this point and level off." He indicated a spot on the graph. In a few minutes the pen came to the indicated point and did not go above that point. Seven minutes later Fermi ordered the rod out another foot.

Again the counters stepped up their clicking, the graph pen edged upwards. But the clicking was irregular. Soon it leveled off, as did the thin line of the pen. The pile was not self-sustaining—yet.

At eleven o'clock, the rod came out another six inches; the result was the same: an increase in rate, followed by the leveling off.

Fifteen minutes later, the rod was further withdrawn and at 11:25 was moved again. Each time the counters speeded up, the pen climbed a few points. Fermi predicted correctly every movement of the indicators. He knew the time was near. He wanted to check everything again. The automatic control rod was reinserted without waiting for its automatic feature to operate. The graph line took a drop, the counters slowed abruptly.

At 11:35, the automatic safety rod was withdrawn and set. The control rod was adjusted and "Zip" was withdrawn. Up went the counters, clicking, clicking, faster and faster. It was the clickety-click of a fast train over the rails. The graph pen started to climb. Tensely, the little group watched, and waited, entranced by the climbing needle.

Whrrrump! As if by a thunder clap, the spell was broken. Every man froze—then breathed a sigh of relief when he realized the automatic rod had slammed home. The safety point at which the rod operated automatically had been set too low.

"I'm hungry," said Fermi. "Let's go to lunch."

## Second Attempt

Perhaps, like a great coach, Fermi knew when his men needed a "break."

It was a strange "between halves" respite. They got no pep talk. They talked about everything else but the "game." The redoubtable Fermi, who never says much, had even less to say. But he appeared supremely confident. His "team" was back on the squash court at 2:00 P.M. Twenty minutes later, the automatic rod was reset and Weil stood ready at the control rod.

"All right, George," called Fermi, and Weil moved the rod to a predetermined point. The spectators resumed their watching and waiting, watching the counters spin, watching the graph, waiting for the settling down and computing the rate of rise of reaction from the indicators.

At 2:50 the control rod came out another foot. The counters nearly jammed, the pen headed off the graph paper. But this was not it. Counting ratios and the graph scale had to be changed.

"Move it six inches," said Fermi at 3:20. Again the change—but again the leveling off. Five minutes later, Fermi called: "Pull it out another foot."

Weil withdrew the rod.

"This is going to do it," Fermi said to Compton, standing at his side. "Now it will become self-sustaining. The trace will climb and continue to climb. It will not level off."

Fermi computed the rate of rise of the neutron counts over a minute period. He silently, grim-faced, ran through some calculations on his slide rule.

In about a minute he again computed the rate of rise. If the rate was constant and remained so, he would know the reaction was self-sustaining. His fingers operated the slide rule with lightning speed. Characteristically, he turned the rule over and jotted down some figures on its ivory back.

Three minutes later he again computed the rate of rise in neutron count. The group on the balcony had by now crowded in to get an eye on the instruments, those behind craning their necks to be sure they would know the very instant history was made. In the background could be heard Wilcox Overbeck calling out the neutron count over an annunciator system. Leona Marshall (the only [woman] present), Anderson, and William Sturm were recording the readings from the instruments. By this time the click of the counters was too fast for the human ear. The clickety-click was now a steady brrrrr. Fermi, unmoved, unruffled, continued his computations.

## The Curve Is Exponential

"I couldn't see the instruments," said Weil. "I had to watch Fermi evey second, waiting for orders. His face was motionless. His eyes darted from one dial to another. His expression was so calm it was hard. But suddenly, his whole face broke into a broad smile."

Fermi closed his slide rule—

"The reaction is self-sustaining," he announced quietly, happily. "The curve is exponential."

The group tensely watched for twenty-eight minutes while the world's first nuclear chain reactor operated.

The upward movement of the pen was leaving a straight line. There was no change to indicate a leveling off. This was it.

"O.K., 'Zip' in," called Fermi to Zinn who controlled that rod. The time was 3:53 P.M. Abruptly, the counters slowed down, the pen slid down across the paper. It was all over.

Man had initiated a self-sustaining nuclear reaction—and then stopped it. He had released the energy of the atom's nucleus and controlled that energy.

Right after Fermi ordered the reaction stopped, the Hungarian-born theoretical physicist Eugene Wigner presented him with a bottle of Chianti wine. All through the experiment Wigner had kept this wine hidden behind his back.

Fermi uncorked the wine bottle and sent out for paper cups so all could drink. He poured a little wine in all the cups, and silently, solemnly, without toasts, the scientists raised the cups to their lips—the Canadian Zinn, the Hungarians [Leo] Szilard and [Eugene] Wigner, the Italian Fermi, the Americans Compton, Anderson, Hilberry, and a score of others. They drank to success—and to the hope they were the first to succeed.

A small crew was left to straighten up, lock controls, and check all apparatus. As the group filed from the West Stands, one of the guards asked Zinn:

"What's going on, Doctor, something happen in there?"

The guard did not hear the message which Arthur Compton was giving James B. Conant at Harvard, by long-distance telephone. Their code was not prearranged.

"The Italian navigator has landed in the New World," said Compton.

"How were the natives?" asked Conant.

"Very friendly."

# Developing an Atomic Weapon

## By Boyd Norton

At the dawn of World War II, a top secret program known as the Manhattan Project brought hundreds of atomic scientists together in the United States to build an atomic bomb. As author Boyd Norton suggests in the following article on the Manhattan Project, "Failure was unacceptable." Success, he says, was "miraculous." After the bomb was completed and utilized, Boyd notes, the science of atomic energy and its related government funding were directed at further military applications. Only token investments were made into the peaceful uses of this revolutionary energy source.

Boyd Norton was a young boy when the atomic bomb was developed. He grew up to be a nuclear physicist working at a nuclear reactor testing station. He left the field in 1969 and has since established himself as a wilderness photographer and writer.

**A**tomic energy and I grew up together.
   I remember well the headlines and stories. For an impressionable nine-year-old, already a whiz kid in science and determined to be a chemist or physicist, it was all very exciting: an atomic bomb, deriving its enormous energy from a mysterious new process called nuclear fission. Adding to the fascination and mystique was the fact that the bomb had been developed as part of a super-secret project and revealed to the world for the first time with the deadly detonations over [the Japanese cities of] Hiroshima and Nagasaki. In 1945 it all seemed so clear and simple: nuclear fission was to become the energy source of the future. The genius that had gone into creating the atomic bomb could clearly find ways to utilize nuclear power safely for peacetime uses.

   The process of nuclear fission is awesome, beautiful, elemental, and elegant; it gets down to the very roots of the universe. The discovery, exploration, and utilization of nuclear fission is one of mankind's greatest intellectual achievements.

It began in the 1930s, an exciting era for the world of physics. In 1932 Sir James Chadwick discovered the neutron, an ethereal subatomic particle that provided physicists with a means of probing still farther into the mysteries of the atomic nucleus.

In 1939 two Austrian physicists, Otto Hahn and Fritz Strassman, demonstrated that the nucleus of uranium atoms actually split, or fissioned, into two lighter parts when hit by neutrons. Normally, because all positive charges repel each other, the electrical barriers between nuclei are sufficient to prevent them from colliding with each other. But because the neutron carries no charge it can easily penetrate the electrical barrier of the nucleus and splinter the nucleus. More important was the discovery that even a small quantity of uranium could release, through fission, thousands of times more energy than could be derived from combustion or other chemical reactions. Almost immediately the military potential of this new process was recognized.

## An Atomic Weapon

The discovery of nuclear fission took place as World War II was imminent. Much of the initial research was carried out in Nazi Germany, though in time many of the European scientists fled to settle in the United States, the United Kingdom, and Canada. One of those was Leo Szilard, an energetic Hungarian physicist who understood thoroughly the military potential of a fission bomb. Fearing the consequences if Nazi Germany should develop such a weapon (Hilter's war machine had already sealed off the uranium mines of Czechoslovakia), Szilard urged his friend, Albert Einstein, to send a letter to President Roosevelt outlining the potential for the development of a fission bomb. Although Einstein would later regret it, his letter played a pivotal role in moving the Roosevelt administration to embark on a massive government project to build the atomic bomb. Hundreds of the world's top scientists were assembled in top secrecy in perhaps the greatest scientific and engineering undertaking of all time: the Manhattan Project.

The events of the Manhattan Project can best be described as a curious blend of luck, inspired direction, dedicated research, brilliant scientific deduction, and more luck. The obstacles—physical, scientific, and economic—were enormous. Using untried methods on unseen substances with uncertain properties, unknown materials were to be refined by unspecified processes to produce untested components for an unimaginable weapon. Failure was unacceptable.

Considering the timetable of events, the accomplishments of the Manhattan Project were doubly miraculous. Only three years after the discovery of fission the first nuclear reactor was built and tested successfully in a converted squash court at the University of Chicago. A brilliant Italian physicist named Enrico Fermi, whose suggestion in 1934 had led to the discovery of fission, directed this historic experiment in 1942. Three years after the first reactor was operated, an atomic bomb was successfully detonated in the lonely New Mexico desert. In many ways it was like making a successful lunar landing only six years after the invention of the first crude rocket.

## Building the A-Bomb

According to Einstein's formula $E = mc^2$ even a small amount of mass ($m$) inside the atom can be magnified by a huge number ($c^2$, or the speed of light squared) to create enormous amounts of energy ($E$). Theoretically this energy can be released whenever the uranium atom is split. In practice, however, releasing the energy in a bomb was not easy. There were two major challenges to be surmounted.

First, two types of uranium atoms exist, which are chemically identical and difficult to separate. Almost all naturally occurring uranium is U-238 (with 92 protons and 146 neutrons in the nucleus), which does not fission easily and cannot sustain a chain reaction. Its exotic cousin U-235 (with three fewer neutrons) fissions readily and is the active ingredient in the atomic bomb; U-235 is also quite rare, comprising only 0.7 percent of all naturally occurring uranium. In order to develop a bomb, scientists had to increase, or *enrich*, the concentration of the exotic fissionable U-235 and reduce the concentration of the more plentiful U-238. Any amount less than 20 percent enriched U-235 would be too low for the purpose of making an atomic bomb.

The second problem was to manufacture enough U-235—known as a critical mass—for the bomb to ignite. Any amount less than critical mass (approximately 25 pounds) would cause too many neutrons to leak out of the uranium. If, however, enough of the U-235 could be held together for a split second, the temperature would have time to rise to several million degrees Centigrade, at which point the uranium would vaporize and the gases develop enormous pressures. In a fraction of a second the gases would expand, creating a tremendous explosion: the result, a nuclear bomb.

The design of the atomic bomb was surprisingly simple. First two pieces of uranium-235, each less than critical mass, were separated. Then one piece, in the form of a missile or bullet, was propelled toward the other rapidly by high explosives. When the two pieces were slammed together, a critical mass was formed, which instantly initiated the chain reaction and the atomic explosion.

Another type of bomb was made from plutonium, a fissionable man-made element. Because of certain technical complications, however, the critical mass for the plutonium had to be assembled much faster than for U-235. Thus the "gun-type method" used for U-235 could not be used for plutonium. Instead, the subcritical plutonium core, in the form of a sphere, was surrounded by TNT which, when detonated, caused a high-pressure shock wave, which squeezed the plutonium into a dense, supercritical mass. In less than a millionth of a second the chain reaction began and caused an atomic explosion. This is called the "implosion method." The first atomic bomb tested in New Mexico in 1945 was of this implosion type, using plutonium, while the Hiroshima bomb was of the "gun type," using U-235.

With the end of World War II many scientists who had worked diligently on the atomic bomb, along with officials of American corporations who had served as contractors to the Manhattan Project, expected that the money and manpower used for developing the bomb would be redirected toward peacetime uses of fission. But right from the start it seemed nearly as difficult to separate the military atom from the peaceful atom as it had been to separate the fissionable isotope uranium-235 from the nonfissionable U-238.

In 1946 Congress passed the Atomic Energy Act, which established the Atomic Energy Commission (AEC) to develop peaceful atomic programs and the Congressional Joint Committee on Atomic Energy (JCAE) to oversee the AEC's activities. The act also attempted to prohibit any exchange of nuclear technology, even between the United States and her wartime Allies, until international safeguards against nuclear weapons could be established. For a short while after World War II the U.S. had a monopoly on atomic weaponry. But in 1949 the Soviet Union exploded its first nuclear device and the nuclear arms race was on. The AEC gave priority to military research, with only token funding of programs useful to developing nuclear power as a commercial, peacetime source of energy.

# CHAPTER 2

# Atomic Energy in Commercial Use

# Toward Commercial Uses for Atomic Energy

**By Daniel Ford**

Following World War II the U.S. Congress passed the Atomic Energy Act of 1946, establishing the Atomic Energy Commission (AEC) to oversee and regulate the development of nuclear weapons and atomic energy. The future of atomic energy, however, did not look bright. Stockpiles of fissionable materials were nonexistent, focus was on nuclear weapons buildup, and several important scientists expressed pessimism and disinterest regarding the establishment of commercial nuclear power. One man and one program, however, showed that atomic energy could be harnessed for more than just weapons-grade explosives. In 1954 Navy Captain Hyman G. Rickover, working for the Naval Reactors Branch of the AEC, introduced the first nuclear powered submarine. In this selection, Daniel Ford describes the advent of Rickover's unique machine as well as the back-and-forth discussions, statements, and reports of key policy makers and scientists that empowered the laws governing the civic uses of atomic energy. Ford was executive director of the Union of Concerned Scientists from 1971 to 1979.

T he feverish wartime A-bomb effort precluded any diversion of resources for a major study of the peacetime uses of nuclear energy. Toward the end of the war, however, a Manhattan Project task force was appointed to develop a policy on postwar nuclear research. The committee, headed by Dean R.C. Tolman of the California Institute of Technology, was not enthusiastic about commercial nuclear power plants. "The development of fission piles solely for the production of power for ordinary commercial use does not appear economically sound nor advisable from the point of view of preserving national resources [i.e., the limited supplies of fissionable materials]," it concluded.

When the war ended, such restrained assessments were quickly pushed aside in the general euphoria about what *Newsweek* called "the miraculous powers of atomic-fission energy." Instead of reflecting on the horrors visited upon [the Japanese cities of] Hiroshima and Nagasaki or on whether the bombs should have been used in the first place, news reports helped to alleviate the nation's feelings of repulsion and guilt by focusing public attention on the more congenial aspects of "the new force.". . .

## The Atomic Energy Act of 1946

Popular enthusiasm notwithstanding, there was small immediate prospect for the wondrous potential of atomic energy. Although Congress and the Administration wanted, as President Truman said, to "make a blessing" of atomic energy, the Cold War [between the United States and the Soviet Union], as well as bureaucratic, technical and economic obstacles, stood in the way. Testimony before Congress on the potential civilian applications of nuclear energy was inconclusive, and there was much disagreement on the likely timetable for achieving usable power from atomic reactors. There was no disagreement, however, about the ominous military implications of nuclear fission. When it passed the Atomic Energy Act of 1946, Congress addressed itself almost exclusively to these grim issues. The legislation was designed principally to protect "atomic secrets," in order to preserve the United States monopoly on nuclear weapons and nuclear technology, and to establish an "Atomic Energy Commission" that would provide civilian control over nuclear weapons. The Act mentions the peaceful uses of atomic energy in passing.

The Atomic Energy Commission, which was given total control over all aspects of atomic energy, opened its doors for business in August 1946. The A.E.C. was soon overwhelmed by its responsibilities for nuclear-weapons development. Its problems were acute. The agency had inherited from the Manhattan Project a vast empire of laboratories and manufacturing facilities that employed some forty-four thousand people and had almost no central management. (For security reasons, these installations had been scattered throughout the country, many in remote locations where "atomic cities," complete with schools and fire departments, had been run by the Manhattan Project.) Leading scientists had left the Manhattan Project at war's end, and the A.E.C.'s laboratories were in disarray. The uranium mine in the Belgian Congo that supplied the raw material for the American nuclear-weapons program was being rapidly exhausted. The reactors built during the war for manufacturing plutonium were falling apart. The spare parts needed to assemble nuclear weapons were not available.

## Scientific Pessimism

The chairman of the new agency, David Lilienthal, had to report to a shocked President Truman on April 3, 1947, that, contrary to world belief, the United States had *no* stockpile of nuclear weapons ready for use. "There was nothing in the cupboard," Carroll Wilson, the first general manager of the A.E.C., said in [an] interview. As the Cold War proceeded, and especially after the Soviet Union exploded its own atomic bomb in September 1949, the A.E.C. was absorbed in a frantic nuclear-weapons buildup and had little time or resources to devote to the peacetime development of atomic energy. "The power thing was pie in the sky, really," Wilson said. "We knew we had to do something with it, but we just had one hell of a lot of absolutely overwhelming problems. All of the other priorities were higher than nuclear power."

A.E.C. scientists, moreover, told the Commission of a broad array of practical problems that needed to be solved before power-producing reactors could become a reality. Lilienthal was flabbergasted by the pessimism of a draft report on the prospects for civilian nuclear power that was prepared in July 1947 by J. Robert Oppenheimer. Oppenheimer was the leading Manhattan Project physicist, and he was then heading the A.E.C.'s General Advisory Committee, a prestigious group that largely determined A.E.C. policy during its first few years. Arguing that "a realistic evaluation of atomic power" was necessary to counter popular misconceptions, the report stated that "it does not appear hopeful to use natural uranium directly as an adequate source of fuel for atomic power," and that to develop plutonium reactors capable of producing enough fuel for the power industry would take decades.

"Had quite a blow today," Lilienthal wrote in his diary. "The General Advisory Committee drafted a statement that, as written, not only discouraged hope of atomic power in any substantial way for decades, but put it in such a way as to question whether it would ever be of consequence." Revising this draft a few months later, the full advisory committee, which included A.E.C. adviser Glenn Seaborg, tried to be more optimistic, but the best that it could say was that it did "not see how it would be possible under the most favorable circumstances to have any considerable portion of the present power supply of the world replaced by nuclear fuel before the expiration of twenty years."

## A Lack of First-Rate Scientists

The General Advisory Committee saw numerous technical and economic problems that beclouded the future use of nuclear energy, but they had other concerns as well. Physicist Eugene Wigner, who had pioneered some of the early reactor work at Oak Ridge, felt that there was a notable lack of first-rate scientists and engineers in the A.E.C.'s postwar reactor development effort. Enrico Fermi, who had led the early work in nuclear reactors, felt that the reactor program had lost much of its appeal. He regarded the A.E.C.'s highly structured and bureaucratic research effort as cautious and uninspired. After the exciting breakthroughs of the Manhattan Project, the remaining work that needed to be done to develop power reactors appeared relatively mundane—selecting and testing materials, studying the properties of different types of coolants, designing the pumps and valves and instruments that would be used. Nobel prizes are not given to people who do plumbing, even if it is for a nuclear reactor's cooling system, and scientists of the highest caliber automatically dismissed most of the tasks needed for reactor development as hack work that was not for them.

"We despair of progress in the reactor program," Oppenheimer said in 1948, summarizing the views of the General Advisory Committee. But the members of this elite group were not about to give up their own personal scientific careers to do the work themselves. Advisory Committee member Glenn Seaborg was typical of the Manhattan Project scientists. After the war he went directly back to Berkeley to head the research team that was continuing the work that had made him famous: discovering new elements. The A.E.C.'s work on reactor development would never get more than token attention from leading nuclear scientists. . . .

# A Nuclear Submarine

Despite the slow and disappointing progress in reactor development, one small office in the A.E.C. was quietly making giant strides toward the goal of usable power from nuclear fission. This was the Naval Reactors Branch that was working, together with the Navy's Bureau of Ships, to build the first nuclear-powered submarine.

The conventional subs used during World War II had dual propulsion systems: electric batteries, which they used when submerged, and diesel engines that could be used only on the surface (because they needed an air intake and exhaust). The diesels were used to charge the batteries, which meant that the subs had to resurface frequently. The faster the sub traveled when submerged, moreover, the quicker the batteries would run down, which made the subs very slow. Nuclear propulsion was attractive because the sub could stay submerged for long periods—possibly months—and would have enough power to operate at high speeds for pursuit and maneuvering.

Still, nuclear submarines were not a high priority of either the A.E.C. or the Navy. The A.E.C. had its own reactor-development program, and the strongly traditional Navy, which favored surface ships, had a disdain for submarines, nuclear or otherwise. Nuclear submarine development was carried out largely as the personal project of a remarkable Navy captain, Hyman G. Rickover. An Annapolis graduate, and an engineer, Rickover outmaneuvered the two cumbersome bureaucracies for which he worked—he had a dual appointment with both the A.E.C. and the Navy—and single-handedly administered one of the most successful technological development efforts in modern history.

In June 1946, with a delegation of other Naval officers, Rickover went to Oak Ridge, Tennessee, to the Manhattan Project's Clinton Laboratory, which had become one of the principal postwar research-and-training centers in nuclear technology. (Its name was later changed to the Oak Ridge National Laboratory.) After a few months there, Rickover and his team had quickly absorbed the available technical information on potential reactor systems and had begun, with shrewd technical judgment and uncanny bureaucratic skill, to organize a tightly scheduled program to build a nuclear-powered submarine. By 1948, the program was under way, and Captain Rickover was able to predict, in 1950, that the first American shipboard reactor would be built by the end of 1953.

# A Pressurized Water Reactor

From physicist Alvin Weinberg, the leader of the Clinton Laboratory scientists, Rickover picked up the idea of a "pressurized-water reactor"—a water-cooled reactor that would operate under high pressure. The principles of a "PWR," as it was called, were simple, and it could be built compactly to fit into the hull of a submarine. The reactor would be a steel tank that housed a small "core" of uranium fuel. The uranium chain reaction produced heat, and that heat would be used to boil water. The resulting steam would drive a turbine that was directly connected to the propeller shaft of the sub. The energy released by nuclear fission would thereby be harnessed as a power source for the sub's propulsion. Rickover knew that engineering all of this would be complicated, but he felt that it could be done—if he could overcome the inertia of the A.E.C. and the Navy.

The key to success, in Rickover's mind, was the focusing of the submarine-reactor development project on engineering practicalities rather than on abstract scientific research. A.E.C. laboratories, he felt, were captivated by fascinating technical novelties, regardless of their practical significance. They would irresistibly pursue every new technical issue the way dogs sniff down rabbit trails. He wanted an engineering effort that would not be distracted by side issues but would systematically produce the nuts and bolts and pumps and wiring for a pressurized-water reactor that would work. . . .

When it came to the actual building of the first submarine reactor, Rickover wanted precise-scale prototype models tested at the A.E.C.'s remote reactor-testing station in Idaho. He demanded exhaustive checks of the reliability of key components. He wanted every last detail to be worked out. How would the equipment be arranged in the tight confines of the sub? Would maintenance technicians be able to reach all of the equipment they might need to work on? What kind of malfunctions could arise when the reactor was operating? How would such contingencies be handled? To all these questions, Rickover insisted on firm answers.

By January 1954, he had them, and he had the U.S.S. *Nautilus*, the first nuclear submarine. Its pressurized-water nuclear reactor worked perfectly, and its development had produced a set of technical handbooks that laid the foundation for a workable technology to generate power through nuclear fission. The general despair about the prospects for nuclear energy, which had prevailed only a few years earlier, suddenly dissipated.

# The Peaceful Atom

"The United States knows that peaceful power from atomic energy is no dream of the future. That capability, already proved, is here—now, today," President Eisenhower declared, before the U.N. General Assembly, on December 8, 1953. He spoke with euphoria about "atomic power for peace." Instead of enlarging the existing stockpiles of weapons, the President urged that nuclear materials be used "to provide abundant electrical energy in the power-starved areas of the world." He would ask Congress for new laws to make such a program possible. "The United States pledges . . . before the world its determination to help solve the fearful atomic dilemma—to devote its entire heart and mind to find the way by which the miraculous inventiveness of man shall not be dedicated to his death, but consecrated to his life."

Reacting speedily to the President's call, the Congressional Joint Committee on Atomic Energy began drafting new laws to promote peacetime nuclear power. The Atomic Energy Act of 1946 had expressly forbidden private ownership of nuclear materials and had established an absolute government monopoly over nuclear energy. President Truman had considered atomic energy "too important a development to be made the subject of profit-seeking," but the business-oriented Eisenhower Administration wanted the restrictions eased so that private industry could enter the nuclear-energy business. The President nominated Lewis Strauss, a former Wall Street investment banker who had served on the Commission from 1946 until 1950, to be the new chairman of the A.E.C. Unleashing "the genius and enterprise of American business," Strauss announced, was the key to atomic-power development, a proposition that led to a bitter ideological fight with congressional Democrats. They attacked the proposals to open up atomic power to private developers as a "giveaway" to industry that would replace the government monopoly over nuclear energy with a private one. Leading Democrats on the Joint Committee wanted the A.E.C., instead, to build and operate power reactors and sell the electricity to the public.

# The Atomic Energy Act of 1954

The full committee, chaired by Republican Representative Sterling Cole, sided with the Administration, and so did the Republican-controlled Congress, which passed a new Atomic Energy Act on August 30, 1954. Among its principal provisions was the instruction to the A.E.C. to issue licenses to private companies to build and operate commercial nuclear-power stations. A corollary assignment directed the agency to adopt whatever regulations it deemed necessary "to protect the health and safety of the public."

"There are about thirty-one references in the law to the 'health and safety of the public,'" Harold Green, a former A.E.C. attorney and authority on atomic energy law, said in a recent interview. "I counted them once. But there is not a single reference in the legislative history"—the four thousand pages of reports, testimony and debates before Congress relating to the law—"to what those health and safety considerations really were. Nobody really ever thought that safety was a problem. They assumed that if you just wrote the requirement that it be done properly, it would be done properly. . . ."

## Considering an Accident

The only major piece of additional atomic-energy legislation Congress considered focused on a concern that was repeatedly emphasized by prospective manufacturers and operators of nuclear power plants: their liability in the event of a serious accident.

"We cannot exclude the possibility that a great enough fool aided by a great enough conspiracy of circumstances could bring about an accident exceeding available insurance," Charles Weaver, vice-president of Westinghouse, testified before the Joint Committee in 1956. If they had to accept the risk of bankrupting liabilities in the event of an accident, industry representatives told the Committee, they would abandon the nuclear power business.

In order to define the extent of potential liability, the Joint Committee asked the A.E.C. in 1956 to do a study of the consequences of a major reactor accident. The Commission's Brookhaven National Laboratory, on Long Island, reported to the committee in March 1957. The document prepared by A.E.C. scientists, entitled "Theoretical Possibilities and Consequences of Major Accidents in Large Nuclear Power Plants," became known, by its A.E.C. publication number, as "WASH-740."

The Brookhaven scientists considered the hypothetical case of a power reactor located about thirty miles upwind of a large city. The assumption was that it had suffered an accident that had released a major fraction of the radioactive material it contained into the air, which was then carried across the countryside by the wind. In the "worst case," A.E.C. scientists estimated that thirty-four hundred people would die and another forty-three thousand would be injured, and seven billion dollars in property damage would result. The authors insisted that such accidents were improbable, and that the report, in order to determine the upper limit on possible liability, was pessimistic deliberately. "The study must be regarded only as a rough estimation of the consequences of unlikely though conceivable combinations of failure and error and weather conditions; it is not in any sense a prediction of any future condition."

The findings of WASH-740 reinforced industry's concern about potential lawsuits. Lobbyists for the electric-utility companies and their equipment suppliers pressed Congress for legislation to protect them against massive damage claims. Eager to remove all roadblocks to nuclear development, Congress obliged them. It passed the Price-Anderson Act of 1957, whose complex provisions made legal history; they effectively repealed every citizen's common-law right to sue for damages caused by some one else's negligence. In the event of injuries from an "extraordinary nuclear occurence," no one could bring a claim against those responsible for building and operating the ill-fated plant. The companies responsible would be absolved of all liability, no matter what carelessness or recklessness on their part caused the accident.

## The Price-Anderson Act

The Price-Anderson Act did provide that the public would get some compensation in the event of a nuclear accident. The victims would apply for money from a $560-million fund that the A.E.C. and private insurers would establish. However, if damages exceeded that amount, no extra money was provided. The $560 million would be apportioned to the victims, with no obligation on the part of the industry to assume the remaining liability.

The fund established by the Price-Anderson Act was a token gesture. The amount to be put into it had been recommended by Senator Clinton Anderson, who suggested that five hundred million dollars would be large enough to indicate that something substantial would be done for the victims, but not so large as to "frighten the country and the Congress to death" by revealing the magnitude of the potential risk.

The Joint Committee was concerned that discussion of the liability issue would raise a public controversy. It had skipped over the subject when the 1954 Act was being considered. When the liability question was taken up in 1956 and 1957, the matter received scant public attention, however, and Congress worked out the details of the new law with industry lobbyists. The Price-Anderson Act was passed on a voice vote in the House of Representatives, after perfunctory debate, and passed by the Senate without debate. This completed the legal foundation for the new industry.

# The First Nuclear Power Plants

## By Elizabeth S. Rolph

The first commercial nuclear power reactor became operational in Shippingport, Pennsylvania, in 1957. Within ten years, electric utilities proposed several dozen more reactors to the Atomic Energy Commission, ratcheting up the scale of power-producing capability in the process. Issues arose: How close to a population center could a nuclear power plant be located? What was the worst realistic accident that could possibly happen? Could engineered safeguards offer adequate protection against accidents? In the following excerpt from her book, *Nuclear Power and the Public Safety*, author Elizabeth S. Rolph notes that many of the decisions made on these issues were educated guesses at best.

I n 1953 the AEC [Atomic Energy Commission] and the Duquesne Light Company announced they would jointly build a 60 MWe [megawatts electric] power reactor in Shippingport, Pennsylvania. The Shippingport reactor generated power in 1957, becoming the first commercially operating power reactor in the United States. Ten years after the Shippingport announcement, Jersey Central Power and Light Company made an equally historic announcement. After thorough consideration of competitive bids from both fossil and nuclear steam system suppliers, the utility announced it was buying a 640 MWe boiling water reactor from General Electric for its Oyster Creek plant. For the first time, a nuclear plant competed successfully against the full range of generating alternatives. Jersey Central's decision was widely heralded as a watershed in the process of commercializing nuclear energy.

For some time, the AEC and certain of the reactor manufacturers had believed that nuclear technology was sufficiently in hand to be of commercial value. The AEC launched its Power Reactor Demonstration Program partly as a vehicle for subsidizing further reactor development, but also to *demonstrate* to the utilities the viability of the technology. Westinghouse, one of the two principal manufacturers, had a strong developmental base from which to work. With prodding from [Navy Captain Hyman G.] Rickover, that firm had settled on the pressurized water technology (PWR) and produced reliable reactors to power the U.S. nuclear submarine fleet. Again under Rickover's close supervision, Westinghouse undertook to design and build the first full-scale nuclear powered electrical generating plant at Shippingport. In 1957, with Shippingport well underway, Westinghouse contracted with the New England utility consortium and the AEC to build a next-generation plant. Yankee (Rowe, Massachusetts), a 185 MWe reactor, improved upon many of Shippingport's design characteristics.

## Two Major Competitors

The General Electric Company, a major supplier of conventional utility equipment, emerged as Westinghouse's only real competitor in the reactor business. General Electric had an association with nuclear reactors that predated that of Westinghouse. It had operated the plutonium-producing reactors at Hanford, Washington, since the end of World War II. And while its boiling water design (BWR) was not as successful as Westinghouse's pressurized vessel design, General Electric also developed and built submarine reactors for the Naval Reactors branch. In 1957, General Electric entered the commercial power reactor market with a contract to build a 210 MWe demonstration boiling water plant for Commonwealth Edison at Dresden, Illinois.

Once Dresden I was underway, General Electric proposed to base further development efforts upon a strategy of comprehensive and orderly increments. To this end, the company launched Operation Sunrise, a program for the parallel exploration of design alternatives through a series of pilot (experimental) and demonstration (evolutionary) plants that would culminate in a commercially competitive "target plant" by the late 1960s.

General Electric was, however, unable to persuade the utilities to participate in the clearly uneconomic early phases of the program. After several frustrating years of trying, the company abandoned Operation Sunrise and, skipping further development steps, entered the competitive market with its Oyster Creek bid: a turnkey contract [promising complete financing, construction, and testing] to build a full-scale plant at a price it knew to be competitive with fossil fuel.

While General Electric knew what price its fossil competitors commanded and designed the turnkey contract specifically to underbid them, it apparently did not intend to lose money in the long run. What the company did expect was to win utility confidence with its competitive offer and thus gain a toehold in the market. Then, after selling three or so similar plants for small losses, it anticipated moving into the black with additional sales of the same basic 600 MWe design.

Westinghouse quickly followed General Electric's lead, contracting to build two pressurized water reactors in 1965 on a turnkey basis. Between 1963 and 1967, both manufacturers contracted to build a total of twelve turnkey plants. Thereafter, that form of contract was abandoned in the United States.

## Optimism Prevails

By offering turnkey contracts at prices competitive with fossil plants, reactor manufacturers reflected an astonishing assurance that the nuclear technology was very well in hand. To make such an offering, they had to believe that, in spite of the fact that they were proposing a new generation of reactors in the 400–600 MWe range (a range well outside previous experience), no major design, construction, or performance problems would arise to distort their projected costs. Considering that only six commercial reactors using the light water configuration had been completed and were actually generating electricity by 1965, the manufacturers were clearly making such judgments in the absence of much experience.

Nonetheless, optimism prevailed. Between 1963 and 1967, utilities contracted for fifty-nine nuclear reactors, accounting for 30 percent of the total steam electric capacity ordered over those years. Of these fifty-nine reactors, twelve were bought under turnkey contracts. But during the same period, utilities ordered forty-seven reactors under contracts with no turnkey provisions. Their willingness to agree to conventional contract provisions clearly demonstrates that the utilities, like the manufacturers, believed nuclear technology was indeed well in hand and could be relied upon to compete with fossil plants. The AEC, seeing commercialization proceed so rapidly, considered its own development function adequately fulfilled and began phasing out its demonstration program and fuel subsidies. The technology had presumably come of age.

The nuclear reactor's competitive strength lay in its low fuel costs. Between 1961 and 1967 the cost of fossil boiler fuel ranged from about 1.3 mils per kwh [thousandths of a dollar per kilowatt hour] in Wyoming to 7.8 mils per kwh in Vermont, averaging 2.6 mils to 2.8 mils nationwide. By comparison, nuclear fuel costs ranged from 1.1 mils to 1.9 mils per kwh over the same period. And during those years the AEC and the nuclear industry believed cheap radioactive waste disposal techniques could easily be developed, so no additional waste storage or disposal charges were calculated for nuclear plants. Operating and maintenance charges were roughly the same for both types of plants. The reactor's competitive weakness lay primarily in its considerably higher capital costs (which include construction and financing costs). On balance, the cost analysis being done in the early 1960s showed the fossil and nuclear 600 MWe plant to be roughly competitive for areas where the cost of fossil fuels was high.

## Regulation

In addition to the normal costs of construction, operation, and fuel, nuclear plants were subject to unique and potentially costly regulatory requirements that did not apply to fossil plants. Siting constraints requiring generating facilities to be located away from load centers imposed two types of additional costs. First, there would be the cost of installing and maintaining transmission equipment. Second, electricity would be lost in the course of transmission. A further siting consideration was access to cooling water. Nuclear plants produced almost a third again as much waste heat as fossil plants, and hence needed easy access to a large supply of cooling water.

Changing regulatory requirements to require backfitting or new safety features could escalate capital costs substantially. And lengthening lead times and licensing delays that deferred the time when a utility began earning a return on its investment could also jeopardize the nuclear reactor's competitive position.

During the 1950s the fledgling nuclear industry kept a low profile, lobbying little and enjoying a junior partner relationship with the AEC. As nuclear technology entered the marketplace, the industry viewed the additional regulatory costs as potentially ruinous and became an outspoken advocate of an "industry position." Chief among its objectives was to persuade the AEC to relax its opposition to siting in or near metropolitan areas and thereby to make transmission costs for nuclear plants comparable to those for fossil plants. Industry's position was ably summed up in testimony by Westinghouse spokesman Joseph Rengel before the Joint Committee on Atomic Energy in 1967.

> Metropolitan sites for nuclear power reactors can be justified on economic grounds at this time. Further, we believe the plants can now be designed, built, and operated safely in metropolitan areas. At the present, the major obstacle is the lack of definitive requirements for satisfying the AEC regulatory bodies. We think these requirements can be defined now.

As part of the same effort to get economically advantageous siting, utilities wanted access to the coasts, where abundant cooling water was readily available. The West Coast, however, presented special siting problems because of its high level of seismic activity.

Second, the industry pushed hard for a short licensing period with no unexpected delays. A persistent theme in industry testimony before the Joint Committee's 1967 Licensing and Regulation Hearing was that standardization was imminent and that it should lead to a major simplification in the licensing process. Advocates argued that once components or systems had been used and approved in one plant design, they should not need reevaluation in a second. Also, to make licensing requirements predictable and reduce the leverage of the AEC staff in changing plant requirements, the industry volunteered to participate in a joint effort with the AEC to draw up a set of comprehensive, firm standards and criteria to govern siting and plant design.

Third, the industry understandably wanted to preclude the imposition of additional, unexpected costs once a project was underway. Backfitting [modifying operating plants] and ratcheting [tightening design standards on as-yet-unbuilt plants] loomed as serious threats. This was especially true after 1965, when operating experience began to give hints of design deficiencies and the increasing size of the new plants prompted increasing concerns about safety margins.

# Remote Siting

The nuclear industry was particularly concerned about the economic penalties of remote siting. Transmission, including construction and maintenance, cost a utility in the neighborhood of $250,000 per mile, while electricity losses from the line and increased system instability could incur similar additional costs. The importance of transmission costs in a utility's choice of generating alternatives was reflected in a 1962 report by [nuclear consulting firm] Sidney Stoller & Associates that predicted that the additional costs imposed by AEC siting requirements of that date would shift the potential nuclear share of all new generating capacity ordered from 20 to 50 percent to 0 to 20 percent. And, in fact, several utilities had already declined to participate in the Power Reactor Demonstration Program because siting requirements increased costs too much.

Although early in the reactor development process the Commission had adopted no explicit policy requiring very remote siting, remote siting had become accepted practice. The early reactors were all AEC-owned test and plutonium production facilities. These reactors had no containment or any other safety features. But they were small, and security as well as safety dictated they be sited in regions remote enough to make them a negligible hazard. However in 1953, when the Commission debated what reactor commercialization strategy to take, it noted that "the present conservative safety standards followed by the Commission in connection with the design and location of nuclear reactors will require complete reexamination in light of the economics and practicalities of private nuclear power development." Even at this early date, it was probably anticipated that a combination of more operating experience and some system of plant safeguards would allow the Commission to give up its remote siting requirements.

# Engineered Safeguards

The containment structure became the Commission's first required safeguard. It first appeared as a single steel sphere on General Electric's Knoll Laboratory reactor in West Milton, New York and as multiple structures enclosing the reactor and the generating facilities of Shippingport. Later the Commission required all Power Reactor Demonstration Program reactors to be contained in steel-lined structures capable of withstanding the pressures expected from a large primary system rupture. But containment was not openly viewed as a substitute for distance, only as a complement to it.

In 1959 the Commission issued proposed siting guides formally specifying required exclusion and population center (defined as 25,000 or more people) distances based on the reactor's designed power output. The nuclear industry vehemently opposed the guides, arguing that they were unnecessarily conservative.

The Commission modified the guides and reissued them two years later, by which time a major segment of the industry had come to prefer conservative guides to no guides at all. In addition to the traditional exclusion area and population center criteria, the new guides required that reactors be somewhat isolated from low population areas as well. While the guides imposed specific, quantitative siting requirements, the Commission softened their impact substantially by affirming that they could be violated "if the design of the facility [included] appropriate and adequately compensating engineered safeguards."

In 1962, the Commission formally adopted the guides as its Reactor Site Criteria, more commonly referred to by their *Federal Register* title as 10CFR100. Since they were criteria, the provisions of 10CFR100 offered performance standards against which proposed reactor designs could be measured, no definitive specifications or design requirements. To further clarify how the criteria would be applied, the regulatory staff published a Technical Information Document, TID 14844, describing with examples how distance would be calculated. For a standard 600 MWe plant with no safeguards except containment, for instance, the exclusion area radius would be 1.9 miles, the low population area radius 28 miles, and the distance to a population center 36 miles.

The economic trade-offs between remote siting and installing the engineered safeguards available at that time appeared to be obvious. In estimates that were widely circulated during the early 1960s, Harold Vann, vice-president of Jackson & Moreland, put the costs of siting a reactor twenty miles from a load center at about $12 per kilowatt capacity. He computed the costs for the full complement of safeguards at about $10 per installed kilowatt in a standard 600 MWe reactor. Therefore, by using safeguards instead of remote siting, a utility could save $1.2 million on a standard 600 MWe reactor.

## Substituting Safeguards for Remote Siting

Manufacturers and utilities missed no opportunity to argue that safety evaluations should be based on a *combination* of site location and engineered safeguards, not on distance alone. Given the economics, their concerns were quite real. Any utility big enough to absorb a nuclear plant into its system served a metropolitan area and needed a local site. Moreover, in the populous Northeast (the area of greatest market potential), if the distance formulae were honored, most sites would be ruled out entirely. As Westinghouse's John Simpson noted in testimony before the Joint Committee,

> If the true technical and economic advantages of nuclear power are to be realized . . . [plants must] be located in load centers. . . . In our opinion, industry has developed reactor systems and engineered safeguards that should permit the location of large nuclear stations in population centers.

By 1963, Clifford Beck, Deputy Director of Regulation, in his article "Engineering Out the Distance Fact," officially acknowledged that the regulatory staff believed engineered safeguards were sufficiently advanced to substitute for some portion of the distance requirements and would license accordingly.

Substituting engineered safeguards for remote siting raised new and somewhat knotty questions. How should a safeguard be balanced against distance? That is, how many miles, for instance, should a pressure suppression pool buy? How should the effectiveness of an engineered safeguard be judged? What standards of proof should be required to demonstrate the safeguard's capability and its reliability? If the information is not available, who then should provide it? While not addressed explicitly, these questions arose and had to be answered in the course of regular Commission business.

The utilities were primarily interested in knowing what they had to do to locate at the load center. Since no standards defined an acceptable plant design for an urban site, their strategy was to submit an application for an urban site as a means of determining what kind of distance credit they could get for the available array of engineered safeguards. But in spite of continued pressure during the early 1960s, the utilities were unsuccessful in gaining access to truly urban sites.

# No Urban Sites Approved

In 1962, Consolidated Edison applied for a construction permit to begin work on its proposed 1,000 MWe Ravenswood reactor in Queens, New York. The AEC and the Advisory Committee on Reactor Safeguards did not reject the proposal out of hand, but they viewed it with obvious skepticism, and eventually Consolidated Edison announced it was canceling the plant. A year later, the Los Angeles Department of Water and Power requested a construction permit for its proposed 492 MWe reactor at Malibu. If the application had not been killed because of seismic problems, it probably would have faced a stiff challenge on grounds of urban proximity. One last attempt was made in 1966 by a utility consortium called Public Service Electric and Gas Co. which proposed a 993 MWe reactor for a site near Burlington, New Jersey. Again both the AEC and the Advisory Committee on Reactors Safeguards informally indicated strong reservations, and the site was shifted to Salem, New Jersey.

During the 1967 Joint Committee Hearings, Representative Craig Hosmer (Democrat/California), a key member of the committee, inquired of Harold Price, Director of Regulation, "Can you give any specifics about what is needed before the AEC would allow a reactor to be sited in a metropolitan area?" Price's answer was simply, "No sir." He went on to point out that good research data, operating experience, and testing and inspection capabilities were probably minimum prerequisites, and that the AEC had access to none of those capabilities at that time. The Advisory Committee on Reactor Safeguards concurred in the AEC's reservations.

Although no urban sites were approved, the regulatory staff was clearly willing to give some credit for engineered safeguards. During the same year the siting criteria were adopted, Southern California Edison's 400 MWe San Onofre reactor was granted a construction permit. In return for installing a safety injection system of borated water designed to fill the reactor vessel and hold expected fission product releases to 6 percent of their normal value, Southern California Edison was able to reduce San Onofre's exclusion zone from .82 miles to .5 miles and its distance from a major population center from 12.5 to 4 miles. After that, reductions became the rule.

The array of possible safeguards fall into four categories: (1) those that contain the fission products during and after an accident, preventing leakage to the outside, (2) those that reduce the pressure from an accident sufficiently to let the containment work, (3) those that reduce the fission products that *can* leak (filters, for example), and (4) for small accidents, those that reduce the effects of a release (tall stacks, dilution devices, and so on).

By the mid-1960s reactor designs had incorporated examples, albeit sometimes modest, of all four categories. But only a few of these reactors had been completed and none had put any safeguards through the test of a real accident. So apart from laboratory scale experiments and engineering calculations, there was little evidence to demonstrate exactly what the capabilities of these safeguards were or with what reliability they would function. Moreover, lack of operating experience and the generally poor understanding of exactly what course a serious accident might take meant that the uncertainties were compounded.

To compensate for the uncertainties, members of the regulatory staff gave only partial performance credit to safeguards in their accident release calculations, and where possible they also required redundant safeguards. How much credit to give and when redundancy should be required were totally subjective decisions left to the discretion of the project staff and subject to the review of the Advisory Committee on Reactor Safety and the Atomic Safety and Licensing Boards.

## Siting Near Seismic Areas

Applications to site reactors on California's seismically active coast presented the regulatory staff with similarly difficult decisions. In an area where water was particularly scarce, coastal siting appeared to be an economic imperative. But there was considerable uncertainty about how to identify an active fault area, about what kinds of stresses a quake actually exerted, and about what given structural designs could actually protect against. Probably because the proposed coastal sites were somewhat removed from population centers, the regulatory staff and the Advisory Committee on Reactor Safeguards responded with more ambivalence to the possibility of siting in seismic areas. But because the licensing progressed further, these cases also provided the opportunity for the first rumblings of citizen opposition to nuclear power.

In 1962, Pacific Gas and Electric (PG&E) applied for a construction permit for a 325 MWe boiling water reactor at Bodega

Head, a site fifty miles north of San Francisco and very near the San Andreas Fault. The staff argued that while the PG&E design was very likely to be able to withstand any expected quake activity, its adequacy could not be empirically demonstrated. In its report of October 26, 1964, the staff therefore concluded that the site was not suitable and that a large reactor should not be the subject of a "pioneering construction effort based on unverified engineering principles, however sound they may be." The staff went on to recommend that the permit be denied. The Advisory Committee on Reactor Safeguards, on the other hand, believed that the engineering principles and general design for the proposed plant suggested it could withstand the forces expected from a quake in the fault zone. The committee was therefore sufficiently assured it could be operated "without undue hazard" to recommend that the commissioner approve PG&E's permit application.

## A New Form of Opposition

While the Advisory Committee and the regulatory staff were trying to resolve their differences, PG&E encountered unexpected opposition from a totally new quarter, a local citizens' group. The Bodega Head Association, a small group organized to oppose the construction permit, initially objected to the plant because the Association opposed development of the unique coastal area. Only later, as its support and the intensity of its campaign grew, did the association add the seismic characteristics of the site to its list of concerns. Surprised by such intense local opposition, PG&E finally abandoned its plans for Bodega Head in November of 1964 and agreed to work jointly with the Sierra Club to find an acceptable alternative coastal site.

A year after PG&E applied for its construction permit, the Los Angeles Department of Water and Power submitted its application for the Malibu plant, also to be located on the coast in an active seismic area. In this case the Advisory Committee on Reactor Safeguards and the regulatory staff agreed that the design was adequate and that a construction permit should be issued. But once again the utility encountered unexpectedly stiff opposition on the seismic issue from the community. Five intervenors contested the permit, including comedian Bob Hope (a participant repeatedly noted in the AEC references to the case, therefore, presumably one to be reckoned with).

In 1966, after protracted hearings, the Atomic Safety and Licensing Board handed down a split ruling allowing the Los Angeles Department of Water and Power to proceed on the basis of a provisional construction permit but also requiring that it strengthen the seismic characteristic of the plant design. In 1967, both the regulatory staff and the intervenors appealed the ruling to the Commission. The Commission's final decision supported the intervenor's contention that the applicant's design had to meet more stringent specifications and then be reevaluated before a permit could be issued and construction begun. The Los Angeles Department of Water and Power then withdrew its application and abandoned the project.

During the same period, Southern California Edison received a construction permit for its 400 MWe San Onofre reactor to be built on the coast next to San Clemente after only minor intervention and an AEC study of the surrounding geology. Then, in 1967, PG&E applied for and, after a contested hearing, was granted a construction permit for Diablo Canyon, its 965 MWe plant on the coast west of San Luis Obispo. At both San Onofre and Diablo Canyon there was clear evidence of seismic activity in the vicinity, though neither location was thought to be in a major fault area.

Thus the regulatory response to the uncertain hazards of siting reactors near seismic areas appeared to be very similar to that of siting in urban areas. While the various regulatory decision groups (the regulatory staff, the Atomic Safety and Licensing Boards, the Commission, and the ACRS) were sympathetic to economic necessities and never suggested that commercial use of nuclear power should be discontinued until the uncertainties were resolved, their decisions reflected the very real technical uncertainties and a perceived need for a certain degree of conservatism. Their assessments were also clearly subjective and qualitative.

# The Early Economics of Atomic Energy

## By Gerard H. Clarfield and William M. Wiecek

As more and more nuclear power plants came on line, the economic story became one of optimistic projections versus reality. As Gerard H. Clarfield and William M. Wiecek claim in the following selection, the Atomic Energy Commission's optimistic predictions of cheap nuclear-generated electricity were based on assumptions about the efficiency of larger power plants and future technologies that did not quite manifest. Various price shocks in the fossil fuel industry, however, kept atomic energy in the marketplace as a possible, viable energy option. Gerard H. Clarfield and William M. Wiecek are currently professors of history at the University of Missouri and Syracuse University, respectively.

The economics of America's first commercial nuclear power plant, Shippingport [in Pennsylvania], were dismal: it produced electricity at a cost of 64 mills [one thousandth of a dollar] per kilowatt hour at a time when conventional coal-fired plants were producing at 6 mills per kilowatt hour. But rather than daunting nuclear proponents, these figures only stimulated them to demand greater government support for the infant industry. . . . Joint Committee [on Atomic Energy] Democrats, municipal utilities, and rural electric cooperatives continued to demand a more active federal role in developing commercial nuclear power, while in the AEC [Atomic Energy Commission] and in industry, the ideological stance of [AEC Chair] Lewis Strauss predominated. Strauss remained convinced that the federal role should be limited to removing impediments to wholly private reactor development. . . .

## The World Need for Atomic Power

A curious combination of Democrats and the infant nuclear industry circumvented this ideological deadlock in an extraordinary way, and thereby gave nuclear development a stimulus great enough to overcome the forbidding economics of Shippingport. The lone Democrat left on the AEC, Thomas Murray, heralded the new approach in 1957 when he called attention to the foreign-policy implications of domestic commercial reactor policy: "Industry's time schedule" for developing nuclear power, Murray argued, "is set primarily by this country's need for electric energy. But the time schedule required by the national interest is much shorter. It is set by the crisis in nuclear weapons and the world need for atomic power."

A policy outline for exploiting that "world need for atomic power" was already in place: [President Dwight] Eisenhower's Atoms for Peace proposal of 1953. The domestic deadlock over reactor policy was broken by American penetration of foreign reactor markets. American nuclear promoters found a transnational structure at hand, ready for their exploitation: Euratom. Beginning in 1955, the principal nations of western Europe, including Great Britain, France, Belgium, and Italy, began discussions looking toward formation of a "European Atomic Energy Community." Italy had the most urgent need for new sources of electricity, Great Britain the most advanced reactor development program, and France the most ambitious combined military-civilian program, thanks to [French President] Charles de Gaulle's desire for a French nuclear weapon. . . . A three-man commission, promptly called by journalists "The Three Wise Men" and headed by the president of the French National Railroad, Louis Armand, toured the United States, Canada, and Great Britain as well as several continental countries in 1957. They submitted a report titled *A Target for Euratom*, calling for a vast increase in European nuclear generating capability and recommending close cooperation with the United States in nuclear matters. The six members of the European Economic Community (the Common Market), accepted these recommendations when they ratified the Euratom treaty shortly afterward.

## Americans Capture the European Market

*A Target for Euratom* was an open invitation for American penetration of the European market. Four members of the U.S. Atomic

Energy Commission supplied essential data and heavily influ-
enced the report. The struggle for the European market that it announced involved a competition among technologies as well as
economies. The two principal American nuclear vendors, General
Electric and Westinghouse, were promoting light water reactors—
the boiling water reactor and the pressurized water reactor respectively. The British and French, by contrast, had constructed gas
graphite reactors. The American vendors vigorously and optimisti-
cally predicted technical and economic success for their largely
untried light water reactor (LWR). The European commission
lacked technical advisers and operating experience to challenge
American claims. Meanwhile, the United States was concluding
bilateral agreements with individual nations and with Euratom,
calling for construction of American LWRs, projected to equal a
thousand megawatts of installed capacity in the 1960s. The United
States government indirectly provided financial support to the
American vendors through low-interest Eximbank [Export-Import
Bank] loans, guarantees of supply and performance of enriched
uranium fuel, and contributions to join research and development
programs. The total amount of America's subsidies for Euratom
came to about half its budget. Euratom thus became, in the evaluation of [authors] Irvin Bupp and Jean-Claude Derian, a "Trojan
horse" by which American vendors captured the European market with LWRs. The Trojan horse enjoyed immediate success,
with orders promptly coming in for American reactors at Chooz,
France, Gundremmingen, West Germany, and Garigliano, Italy.
The principal German nuclear vendor, Siemens, thereupon lost its
interest in gas graphite reactors and announced its conversion to
light water. These events cemented the American vendors' hold
on the European market, and enabled them to play off American
and European developments against each other in a tour de force
of marketing strategy. This stimulated a boom for American light
water reactors that industry experts have since called the "Great
Bandwagon Market."

## Optimistic Predictions

In November 1962, the AEC staff prepared a report, entitled *Civilian Nuclear Power: A Report to the President—1962*, and sent it
to President John F. Kennedy. In it, the AEC noted that the cost of
nuclear-generated electricity was then at about 10 mills/kwh, and

predicted that it would soon fall to nearly half that, 5.6 mills/kwh at Pacific Gas & Electric's projected Bodega Head reactor in California. By 1980, the AEC expected generating costs to fall further, to about 3.8 mills/kwh. (It is a revealing commentary on the reliability of such predictions that the actual 1980 generating costs were 2.3 *cents*, a 600 percent increase.) The report suggested that only modest government assistance, in the form of direct subsidies, would be necessary to carry nuclear power across the threshold of economic competitiveness with fossil fuel-fired plants. These optimistic predictions were based on a number of assumptions:

1. The future economic performance of essentially untried high-technology ventures could be predicted accurately, even where these predictions were for plants three times the size of any that might provide a base of operating experience, and even where auxiliary supporting industrial technologies were just as untried.

2. The scaling-up process would achieve significant economies of scale.

3. "Learning experience" would further reduce costs as engineers perfected designs and procedures on the basis of operating experience.

Each of these assumptions soon proved to be unfounded. Bupp and Derian sardonically observed in restrospect that "the distinction between empirically supported fact and expectation—often quite obviously self-interested expectation—was blurred from the beginning."

## Oyster Creek's a Loss Leader

Reality, however, promptly seemed to vindicate the optimism of the AEC report. In December 1963, Jersey Central Power and Light, a New Jersey utility, signed a contract with General Electric to purchase a 515 MWe [megawatts electric] boiling water reactor for a proposed power plant at Oyster Creek, New Jersey. Jersey Central justified its decision on the grounds that the nuclear plant would produce electricity more cheaply than a comparable coal-fired plant. The Oyster Creek contract proved to be historic: It seemed to announce to the world that nuclear generation of electricity had be-

come competitive with fossil fuels. The rosiest dreams of the nuclear community seemed about to be realized. An entirely new
power source had come into existence; it promised to deliver electricity more cheaply than people had dared hope a decade earlier;
and it did so without the pollution, transportation problems, and labor controversies that bedeviled coal. Lewis Srauss's prediction of
the 1950s now appeared to be within reach: nuclear plants would
deliver electricity "too cheap to meter."

The Oyster Creek contract was remarkable in several respects,
all of which enhanced its dramatic impact. To begin with, it was a
turnkey contract: that is, GE promised to deliver and build a power
plant at a guaranteed price, adjusted only by an inflation escalator.
The buyer need only turn the key to the front door, like a new
homeowner carrying his bride across the threshold, walk in, start
up the machinery, and begin producing electricity. The prime con-
tractor assumed responsibility for the charges of sub-contractors.
All the risk lay with the nuclear supplier. The economics of this
arrangement for the utility looked so promising that shortly the industry predicted that generation costs would immediately drop
even below the low 1962 AEC figures; specifically, from something in the neighborhood of 6.0–7.5 mills/kwh to a breathtaking
4.3 mills for Oyster Creek. Bupp and Derian laconically comment
on these figures: "In keeping with the standards of skepticism established during the debate on the 1962 AEC report, the fact that
the latter figure was expectation and not accomplishment was not
the object of widespread attention."

Industry analysts have concluded that Oyster Creek, and probably at least the next five commercial reactors, were what retail
merchants call "loss leaders": a product sold at or below cost to
lure buyers into the store, where they will probably purchase
something else. Oyster Creek validated the AEC's optimism; it
pushed the Europeans along in their decision to abandon gas
graphite and other reactor types for the American LWRs; and,
above all, it presented claims of economic performance so impres-
sive that the bandwagon effect began.

## The Great Bandwagon Market

Within five years of the Oyster Creek order, American utilities
alone had placed orders for seventy-five new nuclear plants having over 45,000 MWe generating capacity. Installed capacity (that

is, reactors actually built and on line) by 1975 approached 100,000 MWe. The growth of nuclear power in the United States was proceeding along an exponential curve. Hope and reality, at first mutually reinforcing, became indistinguishable. Normally sober men spoke of a Promethean future. Alvin Weinberg, director of the Oak Ridge National Laboratory, hailed the "nuclear energy revolution" that would provide a "permanent and ubiquitous availability of cheap power." Promise beckoned reality, then substituted for it, while reality elicited ever more dazzling expectations. In these unreal expectations, the engineering equivalents of watered stock, the Great Bandwagon Market in retrospect eerily resembles the Great Bull Market on Wall Street from 1927 to 1929.

In all this, utilities were taking a high risk, measured by the distance between actual operating experience and extrapolated estimates. This represented a revolutionary change in management practices. Previously the electric power industry considered even an extrapolation as low as 2:1 over experience as risky; during the Great Bandwagon Market, this ratio moved recklessly up to 4:1. At the end of the Bandwagon era in the late 1960s, the ratio of ordered to operating capacity soared from 2:1 to 30:1. More than ignorance, greed, and folly account for this. In the 1960s, nuclear power remained a "sexy" technology, in an era when few questioned either the premises or the promises of high technology. A talented and ambitious engineer or business-school graduate might well have regarded coal as a dull, frumpy, uninteresting career option. At a time when men dreamed of nuclear rocket and aircraft propulsion, when many saw nuclear power as the only sure and ultimate guarantor of our national existence, the glamour of the industry provided its devotees an unusually intense stake in its success. Engineers and scientists had an emotional commitment to achieving the success of nuclear power, something that went beyond the mere self-interest of the sort that aims at keeping the paychecks coming in. They were, in Alvin Weinberg's unforgettable phrase, the "nuclear priesthood," oddly reminiscent of the ancient Egyptian priestly caste that retained its power at the pinnacle of its society by reason of its monopoly of the arcane lore of astronomy and mathematics, which they used to predict the annual flood patterns of the Nile. Nuclear science and technology had been spectacularly successful, and few were prepared to hang crepe about its future.

Economic considerations played a role, too. Private utilities had been so frightened by Democratic talk in the previous decade of nuclear TVAs [Tennessee Valley Authorities] that they jumped on the bandwagon to prevent a public-power preemption of nuclear power. (TVA itself, the real TVA, placed orders for two large units, Browns Ferry 1 and 2, each 1,000 MWe, early in the Bandwagon era.) Finally, the vicious circle of industry basing its predictions on AEC assertions, and the AEC basing its claims on industry predictions, produced "a circular flow of mutually reinforcing assertions that . . . inhibited normal commercial skepticism about advertisements which purported to be analyses."

Reality quickly intervened. Capital and operating costs did not fall as predicted; on the contrary, they rose stubbornly. Just as stubbornly, the AEC and nuclear vendors claimed that "stabilization" was just around the corner, that uncertainties would soon vanish, that experience, economies of scale, and engineering improvements would shortly set costs on a predictable, downward curve. Moreover, AEC economists masked or excused the failure of their predictions by claiming that competitive costs, especially for coal, moved in tandem with nuclear costs so that nuclear power still remained relatively competitive. But events on the other side of the globe would shortly relieve the nuclear industry of these frustrating uncertainties.

## The Arab Oil Embargo

From 1971 through 1974, a series of shocks deranged the economics of electric utilities. The best remembered is the Arab oil embargo of 1973. After the outbreak of the Yom Kippur War, Egypt's Arab supporters in OPEC (the Organization of Petroleum Exporting Countries) declared an embargo on their oil exports to the United States and the Netherlands. The effect was instantaneous and dramatic: gasoline and heating oil prices shot up, long lines formed at gas stations, distributors and state governments were forced to experiment with various measures to restrict the purchase of gas, such as odd/even date purchase restrictions or minimum five-dollar purchase requirements. In 1970, the U.S. imported Arabian light crude at around $2/barrel; by the end of 1973, that price had jumped to nearly $12, a 600 percent increase. The Arab oil embargo struck Americans directly where they were most vulnerable: in their relationship with their autos.

Surging gas prices at the pump were symptomatic of a steady

increase in all energy prices. Residual fuel oil was tied to the OPEC prices and it rose with them, hitting residents of the east coast hardest because of their dependence on imported oil for domestic heating. Coal and natural gas prices followed along, coal being stimulated by increased costs caused by enforcement of the Clean Air Act of 1970 and a brief mineworkers' strike. These rising fossil fuel prices saved the economic position of nuclear power.

## Nuclear Power Versus Coal

A fundamental proportion underlies the economic competitiveness of fossil and nuclear generating plants. Relative to each other, fossil plants have low capital costs but high fuel costs and high operating-and-maintenance costs; nuclear plants present high capital costs but low fuel costs, plus low O&M costs. . . . Moreover, the capital costs were rapidly becoming unpredictable at the time of the 1973 oil embargo because of cost escalation and interest rates. Nearly half the capital cost of a 1,000 MWe nuclear plant, with costs estimated in 1974 and projected start-up in 1983, was attributable to interest and escalation (17 percent and 30 percent respectively). Fossil plants would suffer from the same uncertainties of the capital markets, too, but their lower initial capital costs and shorter construction time made this component relatively less important.

The upshot of all this is that for nuclear generation to remain competitive with coal, nuclear fuel costs must remain low and stable. Where nuclear's capital costs shoot up, as they did in the decade 1963–1973, this rise must be offset by an equally drastic rise in fossil fuel costs. That is exactly what the Arab oil-exporting countries provided the United States in 1973. Had imported crude prices remained at their Garden-of-Eden 1970 levels, nuclear power would not have been near a competitive position with fossil fuel and the industry would have died at birth. As it is, only massive life-support systems, in the form of federal subsidies, have kept the infant breathing so far.

As the 1970s wore on, the economics of the nuclear power industry did not improve, and subsidies plus ballooning fossil fuel prices were necessary to keep nuclear in the game. Nuclear's position was mauled further when its fuel costs rose. In 1972, the spot market price for yellowcake, a form of processed uranium oxide, was unnaturally low, somewhere between six and eight dollars a pound. This came about largely because Westinghouse in the Bandwagon days had committed itself to numerous long-term contracts as a uranium-buying agent to supply yellowcake at low prices in order to provide an incentive for utilities to buy its pressurized water reactors. This was a high-risk, economically irrational gamble, but Westinghouse persisted in it until by January 1975 it had gone 40,000 tons short on its commitments. By December of that year, yellowcake prices had risen five-fold, to somewhere around $35/lb. Claiming that it faced potential losses of $2 billion, Westinghouse announced in September 1975 that it would not honor its supply contracts, arguing that it was released from its contractual obligations by reason of "commercial impracticability" under section 2-615 of the Uniform Commercial Code. Twenty-seven utilities promptly sued, and the litigation provided one of the most significant modern episodes of commercial law development in recent times, both by reason of its magnitude and because it presented a dramatic opportunity to test the meaning of section 2-615. . . . But the sudden and shocking rise in fuel prices was simply another blow to an industry that could only look back wistfully on its Bandwagon era.

While the industry was undergoing its painful confrontation with market reality, the AEC was beginning to overcome its adversarial posture toward the JCAE [Joint Committee on Atomic Energy] and to establish policies for civilian nuclear power that were to have important long-term consequences. Under the Atomic Energy acts, the AEC had both promotional and regulatory roles. It had a mandate to develop and encourage nonmilitary applications, yet at the same time, its responsibilities for public safety and health created a tension in its functions that it never satisfactorily resolved. As early as 1961, when the Commission had been functioning only fifteen years, concerned observers of the regulatory process recommended that it be split, with one branch being responsible for promotion and operations, and the other for regulation, licensing, and standards. Its military responsibilities only complicated this dual role, with disastrous results.

## An Atomic Consortium

The AEC became part of what David Lilienthal, its first chairman, called "an atomic consortium, that is, groups of bureaucracies in private and public life that have a vested career interest in the status quo and that guard their reputations and privileges as zealously as any other 'establishment.'" This establishment formed what political scientists informally call "the iron triangle":

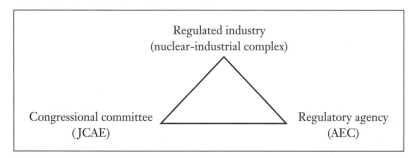

Regulated industry
(nuclear-industrial complex)

Congressional committee
(JCAE)

Regulatory agency
(AEC)

But the picture is more complicated than this simple diagram would suggest. For one thing, there is a fourth element, necessitating a quadrangular sketch: the research and academic groups, consisting of scientists and engineers at the National Labs and the other federal nuclear facilities, as well as the departments of nuclear and chemical engineering at the nation's larger universities. In fact, some of the universities, most notably the University of California at Berkeley, are themselves an inherent part of the establishment because of their position as academic contractors. (At one time, the Lawrence Livermore weapons laboratory and the Los Alamos Scientific Laboratory were both operated under Berkeley's auspices.) Industry itself is not a monolith, as the dispute between Westinghouse and its yellowcake buyers indicates. The increasingly close relations between the AEC and the JCAE, amicable to the point of being incestuous, succeeded the asperities of the Strauss era and blurred the distinctions between the two bodies.

# The Soviet Atomic Energy Program

## By Zhores A. Medvedev

In the following selection, author Zhores A. Medvedev provides a brief history of the former Soviet Union's atomic energy program. Medvedev was a scientist who was expelled from the Soviet Union in 1973. His account provides a bit of insight into the Cold War mindset on the Soviet side. For example, Soviets believe the first nuclear power station was the Obninsk AES (Atomic Energy Station) near Moscow. Westerners believe it was the Calder Hall station in Britain. Furthermore, the Soviets gave priority to the "reactor, high-boiling, channel-type" reactor, partly because any other was considered too imitative of Western models.

Although the Soviet Union was the third country to make an atomic bomb (the British bomb preceded it), it was the first to adapt nuclear reactors to produce electricity. Soviet nuclear scientists are proud of their pioneering role in the peaceful use of nuclear energy. An experimental nuclear power station, now known as Obninsk Atomic Energy Station (AES), began generating electricity on 27 June 1954. It was an integral part of the Physico-Power Institute, now the largest centre of reactor technology in the Soviet Union and responsible for the design and development of many subsequent types of reactor including the pressurized-water reactors for ships and submarines and the fast breeders. It is commonly thought in the Soviet Union that Obninsk AES was the world's first nuclear power station. It was here, they believe, that the problem of controlling the fission reaction of uranium, necessary to produce electric power, was resolved.

In fact, many Western experts dispute this claim. The small, experimental Obninsk AES (about 5 MWe) had no commercial value. Its own electrical needs (for water pumps and other systems) probably consumed more than it produced and it drew electricity from the general grid of the Moscow energy network. They take the Calder Hall 50 MWe reactor as the first real nuclear power station. Calder Hall was switched into the British national grid on 17 October 1956, amid much international publicity. But even Calder Hall was merely the first power reactor that the public knew about. There was no publicity for the first American and Soviet power reactors.

Obninsk, which is 100 km south of Moscow, is closed to foreigners. In 1954 it was not a town in the conventional sense, but a secret prison-camp facility where prominent Soviet scientists worked alongside German physicists who were still prisoners-of-war. A prison labour camp was attached to the research centre. Construction and other work on the site were largely done by the inmates. The settlement had no name in 1954. It was merely a PO Box address, part of a vast empire of military atomic installations and research centres headed by Igor Kurchatov, the father of the Soviet atomic bomb and a legendary figure in Soviet science.

One of Kurchatov's biographers has described how public excursions to the first AES were organized after its existence was officially announced. On 1 July 1954 the USSR Council of Ministers published an announcement "Concerning the Inauguration in the USSR of the First Industrial Power Station using Atomic Energy." It did not reveal the location of the plant and no further details were released for nearly a year.

Kurchatov had submitted a proposal to build a power reactor in 1949. Within a year he had received governmental approval to start work. He appointed D. I. Blokhintsev, who directed the Obninsk Institute, to head the project although he himself supervised everything, including the emergency shutdown mechanisms. Nikolai A. Dollezhal and Anatoly A. Aleksandrov were members of the scientific team. Dollezhal, who was an expert on power stations, completed the blueprints for the power turbine, while Kurchatov chaired discussions concerning the best model of reactor. The alternatives included the gas-cooled system. According to his biographers, Kurchatov himself chose the graphite-moderated, water-cooled model, apparently because it had already been successfully tested for military purposes. During this period plutonium production was the most important economic consideration and designers favoured the models which would yield the most plutonium.

# Secret Research Facilities

No journalists were present at the inauguration of the first AES on 27 June 1954. It was only in 1967, seven years after Kurchatov's death that the event was described. The prison research centre had been dismantled in 1955, when all the remaining German prisoners-of-war and deportees had been released and returned to Germany (a condition for the establishment of diplomatic relations between the Soviet Union and the Federal Republic of Germany). In the West it was public knowledge that German scientists had participated in the Soviet nuclear programme, but it only became known in the Soviet Union in 1987, when D. A. Granin published a biography of N. W. Timofeeff-Ressovsky, a prominent Soviet radiation geneticist who lived and worked in Germany from 1926 to 1945. Granin described the work of a research team of German scientists in the Ural military nuclear centre where they were attached to the plutonium-producing facilities. In 1955 the "laboratory was closed and the Germans were allowed to return home. This surprised them very much: they had expected to have to work much longer for the victorious power." The most prominent German scientists were Professors K. G. Zimmer and N. Riehl. Riehl had been closely involved in Germany's nuclear project in 1941-5. The US Institute of Information *Citation Index* shows a gap in Riehl's publications between 1941 and 1956.

The secret research facilities at Obninsk only acquired the name Obninsk in 1958, when the name first appeared on Soviet maps. Several other research institutes were established in the town. In 1962 the Research Institute of Medical Radiology was established and I was invited to set up its molecular radiobiology laboratory. I lived in Obninsk for nearly ten years. It was (and probably still is) a very pleasant town. Everybody who lives and works in an atomic centre like Obninsk acquires a more than superficial knowledge of the details of atomic energy, despite the obsession of local officials to preserve the secrecy of everything linked to atomic research.

Between 1974 and 1980, while living in Britain, I visited the principal nuclear research centres in the United States: the Argonne, Brookhaven, Oak Ridge and Los Alamos National Laboratories. At none of them did I see such elaborate security systems as those at Obninsk, where more than a battalion of professional military guards with dogs patrol a system of multiple fences and electrified wires separated by strips of freshly ploughed ground. . . .

## Program Approved

Obninsk remained the only Soviet AES for nearly a decade. Turning an experimental nuclear power reactor into an economically viable, commercial power station proved difficult. In the 1950s the Soviet Union had more than enough sources of cheap energy. Constructing military plutonium-producing reactors (graphite-moderated) and power reactors for ships and submarines (more compact pressurized-water reactors with the same output) was considered more important than nuclear power stations. In March 1956 Kurchatov advocated the rapid development of power stations. In addition to the two models already tested (later known as the RBMK [reactor, high-power, boiling channel-type] and VVER [in Russian, water-water power] reactors), he was enthusiastic about small reactors which might be used by locomotives and even aeroplanes. He also wanted fast breeders to be developed as the most promising future source of energy.

When the Soviet nuclear energy programme was finally approved by the government sometime in 1956 or 1957, all three reactor types (graphite-moderated, pressurized-water and fast-breeder) were included in the programme. It was not because of economic efficiency, safety or institutional support that the RBMK was later given priority. In the late 1950s and the 1960s it was simply easier for Soviet industry to construct its less sophisticated design. The *diktat* [authority] of producers over consumers, pinpointed by *glasnost'* [openness] as the main weakness of the Soviet economy, was important in giving a technically obsolete model a new lease of life. The Ministry of Power and Electrification, responsible for running nuclear power stations, was given no choice: it could decide design and construction questions concerning turbines, but not reactors. There were also nationalistic reasons for giving priorities to the RBMK system: it was the only entirely Soviet system. Other designs would have entailed copying or imitating Western models.

# Types of Nuclear Reactors

## By Richard Wolfson

In this selection, author Richard Wolfson describes the basic concepts behind the most popular nuclear reactor designs in the United
States, Canada, and Europe. The salient differences among the designs are the substances used as moderator and coolant. The moderator is an element or compound used to sustain a chain reaction
within a nuclear reactor, and the coolant is any fluid used to remove
heat from the reactor and transport it to the reactor's turbine (or en-
gine) where it can be made into useful energy. As Wolfson points
out, each reactor design has strengths and weaknesses, most notably
in terms of safety and its ability (or lack thereof) to make weapons-
grade plutonium as a by-product of normal operation. Wolfson is a
professor of physics at Middlebury College in Vermont.

The essential goal in running a nuclear power plant . . . is to
maintain a steady chain reaction. At the heart of the power
plant is its nuclear reactor, a system engineered to sustain a
controllable chain reaction. . . .

## Neutrons, Fast and Slow

When a neutron hits a uranium nucleus, will it always cause fission?
. . . For low-energy neutrons (also called slow neutrons), only the
isotope U-235 will undergo fission. Nuclei of the more common
isotope U-238 may absorb a neutron, eventually becoming
plutonium-239. High-energy neutrons (fast neutrons) will also fission U-235 and, if fast enough, may even fission U-238. But the
likelihood of fission varies drastically with neutron energy. For U-
235, slow neutrons are several thousand times more likely than fast

Richard Wolfson, *Nuclear Choices: A Citizen's Guide to Nuclear Technology*. Cambridge, MA:
MIT Press, 1991. Copyright © 1991 by the Massachusetts Institute of Technology. All rights reserved. Reproduced by permission.

neutrons to cause fission. Thus it is much easier to achieve a chain reaction if the high-speed neutrons emitted in fission can be slowed. In contrast, U-238 fission requires extremely fast neutrons—even the fast neutrons emitted in fission aren't fast enough. This is why it is not possible to sustain a chain reaction with U-238. . . .

Because slow-neutron fission of U-235 is so much more likely, a chain reaction employing slow neutrons can be sustained in uranium even when a great deal of nonfissile U-238 is present. Even though the U-238 absorbs many of the neutrons, those slow neutrons that do strike U-235 nuclei are very effective in causing fission. A slow-neutron chain reaction may therefore work in uranium with U-235 at its natural abundance of only 0.7 percent, although in many reactors slight enrichment with U-235 is necessary. The use of natural or slight enriched uranium in power-plant reactors is important for two reasons: First, enrichment is an expensive process. Second, natural or slightly enriched uranium cannot be used directly to make nuclear weapons.

The fact that most power reactors use slow neutrons provides an answer to an often-asked question: Can a nuclear reactor blow up like a bomb? The answer, for a slow-neutron reactor, is a definitive No. A bomb gets its destructive power not only from the sheer amount of energy released but also from the suddenness of that release; a typical nuclear bomb explosion is over in a millionth of a second. In a bomb, the chain reaction is sustained by fast neutrons that spend only about ten billionths of a second between being released in one fission event and striking a nucleus to cause another fission event. In a reactor, neutrons take 10,000 times longer between fission events, so even a reactor that was badly out of control could not undergo a bomb-like explosion. That is not to say that a nuclear reactor could not fail catastrophically or even explosively; however, even the most violent reactor disaster would not have an explosive effect approaching that of a nuclear weapon.

## The Moderator

In a nuclear power reactor, slow neutrons sustain the fission chain reaction. But the neutrons released in fission have high energy—they are fast neutrons. Slowing them down is the job of the moderator, a substance that absorbs neutron energy. At the microscopic level, collisions between neutrons and nuclei in the moderator are what slow the neutrons.

When objects collide—whether they be subatomic particles, billiard balls, or cars—the most effective energy transfer occurs if the objects have similar masses. A good moderator, then, is a substance whose nuclei have about the same mass that neutrons have. The single proton in a hydrogen nucleus has essentially the same mass as the neutron, so hydrogen is a good moderator. That makes water ($H_2O$) an appropriate moderator substance, and indeed water is the moderator in nearly all U.S. power reactors. But hydrogen has one failing: It often absorbs neutrons. A moderator should absorb neutron *energy*, but not the neutrons themselves; otherwise it reduces the number of neutrons available to sustain the chain reaction. This loss of neutrons means that water-moderated reactors cannot run on unenriched, natural uranium; there simply aren't enough U-235 nuclei around to sustain a chain reaction with the reduced number of neutrons. So fuel for U.S. power reactors must be enriched, to about 3 percent U-235, to overcome the effect of neutron absorption in the moderator. The expense of enrichment is balanced by the abundance of the moderator substance, water.

After ordinary hydrogen ($^1_1H$), the next heaviest nucleus is deuterium ($^2_1H$, also called D), the hydrogen isotope whose nucleus contains a proton and a neutron. Since its mass is twice that of the neutron, deuterium isn't as efficient at absorbing neutron energy. But it makes up for that inefficiency by having a very low probability of absorbing neutrons themselves. Neutrons in a deuterium-moderated reactor are therefore so abundant that the reactor can run on natural, unenriched uranium despite its low (0.7 percent) proportion of fissile U-235. Since it is chemically similar to ordinary hydrogen, deuterium also combines with oxygen to make water—in this case heavy water ($^2H_2O$, or $D_2O$). Heavy water is present in minute quantities in ordinary water, and can be separated and used as a reactor moderator. The Canadian nuclear program emphasizes heavy-water reactors, or HWRs. (U.S. reactors, in contrast, are called light-water reactors, or LWRs.) Heavy water has been considered a "sensitive material" since the dawn of the nuclear age, since a nation possessing it can make plutonium for bombs without needing enriched uranium.

In some reactor designs, solid graphite—the common form of carbon used in pencil "lead"—serves as the moderator. The carbon nuclei in graphite are much more massive than neutrons but, like deuterium, exhibit very little neutron absorption. Graphite-moderated reactors are used in a number of European power plants; most graphite reactors in the United States produce pluto-nium for nuclear weapons.

People are often confused about the role of the moderator in a nuclear reactor. The name suggests that it moderates—that is, con-trols or tempers—the nuclear reaction. In fact, the opposite is true: The moderator makes the nuclear reaction go. Without the mod-erator, only fast neutrons would be present. In reactor fuel, with its low proportion of fissile U-235, those fast neutrons could not sustain a chain reaction. What the moderator does moderate is the speed of the neutrons; the slow neutrons that result are more ef-fective at causing fission.

## Controlling the Chain Reaction

To keep the chain reaction running steadily, something must main-tain the delicate average of exactly one neutron from each fission causing another fission. If that number—called the multiplication factor—drops below 1, the reaction will fizzle to a halt; if it goes over 1, the reaction will quickly go out of control.

To grasp the disastrous consequences of a rise in the multipli-cation factor, consider a nuclear reactor running at its rated power level of 3,000 MW [megawatts]. Suppose the multiplication fac-tor changes from 1 to 2. Then, in the time—called the generation time—that it takes neutrons from one fission to cause another, the rate of fissioning will double, and the reactor's power will increase to 6,000 MW. Another generation time and it will be 12,000 MW; one more, and it will be 24,000 MW—8 times what the power plant is designed to handle, and sure to cause violent destruction. A multiplication factor of 2 is unrealistic, but suppose it gets just a little above 1—say, 1.01. Then after one generation the power level will be 3,000 MW × 1.01, or 3,030 MW. After two genera-tions, it will be 3,030 MW × 1.01, or 3,060 MW. Carrying this procedure through 10 generations gives a power level of 3,314 MW (still tolerable) but after 100 generations the power has nearly tripled, exceeding 8,000 MW. And after 500 generations, the re-actor power has risen to nearly 150 times its design value. Since the generation time is only a fraction of a second, a multiplication factor even a little over 1 can quickly lead to disaster.

Controlling a nuclear reactor means keeping the multiplication factor—the number of neutrons from each fission that cause sub-sequent fission—at *exactly* 1. This is done by inserting neutron-absorbing material, in the form of control rods, between the uranium fuel rods. If the multiplication factor rises above 1, the control rods are inserted further to absorb more neutrons and thereby lower the multiplication factor. Should the multiplication factor drop below 1, the rods are withdrawn to provide more fission-causing neutrons and thus maintain the chain reaction. Control rods also adjust the power output of the reactor, and can be inserted to halt the chain reaction. An emergency shutdown, or scram, occurs when the control rods are inserted fully into the reactor. Reactors are generally designed to scram automatically whenever a potentially dangerous situation arises . . .

What if a reactor does get out of control—can we be sure the control rods will have time to react? Even a slow neutron takes only $\frac{1}{10,000}$ second from its release in one fission event until it causes another fission. At that rate, the 500 generations of neutrons that blew up our 3,000-MW reactor a few paragraphs ago would be over in less than $\frac{1}{10}$ second. No mechanical system can possibly respond in that time. Fortunately, reactor control *is* possible, thanks to the fact that a very few neutrons are released not in the fission event itself but in the subsequent decay of fission products. The effect of these delayed neutrons is to make the average generation time about $\frac{1}{10}$ second. That means it takes a relatively long time for a reactor's power to increase significantly if the multiplication factor rises slightly above 1, so there is enough time for mechanical control rods to operate.

Even with delayed neutrons, care in reactor engineering and operation is essential. Control is maintained as long as the reactor has its multiplication factor so close to 1 that the chain reaction wouldn't continue without the delayed neutrons. Then slight variations result in slow changes in reactor power, and the control rods can respond to these changes. But if the multiplication factor goes high enough that the so-called prompt neutrons alone can sustain the reaction, the generation time becomes much shorter and the reaction may go rapidly out of control. This is precisely what happened at Chernobyl, where operators inadvertently put the reactor into this situation of *prompt criticality*. The reactor power then soared to 500 times its design value in only 5 seconds.

Fission in a nuclear reactor produces heat. Unless that heat is removed, the reactor's temperature will continually rise, possibly resulting in a meltdown. In a power reactor, of course, we want to get the heat out of the reactor in the form of high-energy steam to turn the turbine-generator. Removing heat from the reactor is the job of the coolant, a fluid that circulates through the reactor to pick up heat energy and transport it where it can be useful.

Coolants, like moderators, vary with reactor design. In U.S. light-water reactors, ordinary water is the coolant. The same water, in fact, serves as both coolant and moderator. This is an important safety factor, since a loss of coolant also means a loss of moderator. With no moderator, the fission chain reaction comes to a halt. There is still the danger of meltdown, since the decaying fission products generate considerable heat, but the power level is well below that of the chain reaction itself. In addition to ordinary water, coolants used in commercial slow-neutron reactors include heavy water and the gases helium and carbon dioxide.

## Reactor Designs

All slow-neutron reactors share the three common features that have just been discussed: moderator, control rods, and coolant. Working with those three elements, nuclear engineers around the world have developed very different reactor designs. The details of those designs are not just for engineers, since they have direct bearing on the public debate over the safety of nuclear power. A brief overview of the reactor designs commonly used in nuclear power plants follows.

## Boiling-Water Reactor

Asked to design a nuclear reactor, you might imagine putting pieces of uranium fuel in a container of water. Circulating around the fuel, the water would slow neutrons to maintain a chain reaction, and would simultaneously absorb heat. The water would boil, and the resulting steam could run a turbine-generator. That, in a nutshell, is a boiling-water reactor, or BWR—in many ways, the simplest design for a power reactor. Your BWR-based power plant might look something like figure 1.

About one-third of U.S. nuclear power reactors are BWRs. The uranium fuel in these reactors is sealed in long tubes of corrosion-resistant metal, with many tubes joined to form fuel bundles. These bundles, mounted inside the heavy steel pressure vessel, make up the reactor's core. The water that serves as coolant and moderator circulates among the fuel rods. In normal operation, most of the

*Figure 1.* Diagram of a nuclear power plant using a boiling-water reactor. The turbine is turned by steam generated in the reactor vessel itself.

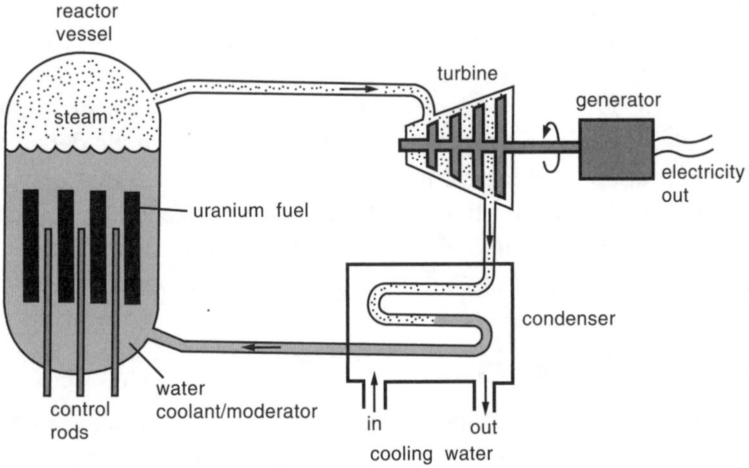

dangerously radioactive fission products remain encased in the fuel. But some gaseous fission products work their way into the water, and, in addition, neutron absorption in the water gives rise to radioactive tritium. For these reasons, the water and the steam circulating through the turbine are radioactive. This means that a break in a steam pipe will release radioactivity, and it also requires radiation protection for workers servicing the turbine.

## Pressurized-Water Reactor

The pressurized-water reactor, or PWR, is a close cousin of the BWR. The main difference is that water in the PWR's reactor vessel is held under such high pressure that it is not able to boil, despite its high temperature. This superheated water goes from the reactor vessel to one or more separate steam generators, where it flows through pipes in contact with water that is allowed to boil. The resulting steam turns the turbine-generator, is condensed back to water, and then returns to the steam generator to complete the cycle. The turbine, the condenser, and the boiling-water part of the steam generator constitute the secondary loop of the cooling system. Water in the secondary loop never comes in contact with the reactor core, so it is not radioactive. Radioactive water is limited to

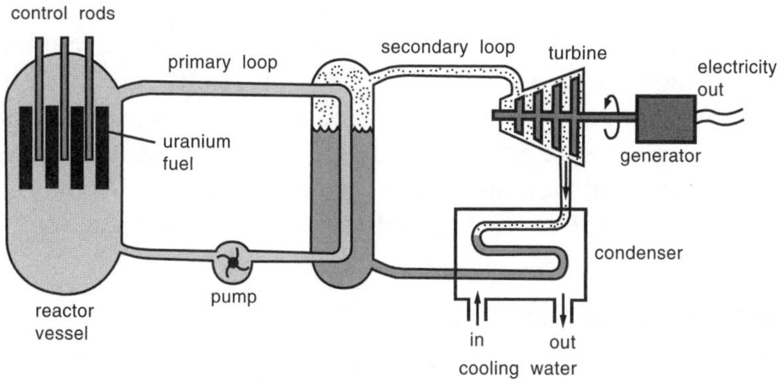

*Figure 2.* Diagram of a power plant using a pressurized-water reactor, showing the primary and secondary coolant loops that share the steam generator.

the primary loop, consisting of the reactor vessel and the primary coolant pipes that flow through the steam generators. Steam generators are mounted close to the reactor vessel, within a thick containment structure; this makes the release of radioactivity unlikely even in the event of a failure in the primary coolant system. Figure 2 shows the essential features of a pressurized-water reactor.

About two-thirds of the commercial nuclear power plants in the United States use PWRs. They have proved more reliable than BWRs, with nine of the top ten long-term performance records going to PWRs. On the other hand, the most significant reactor accident in the United States—that at Three Mile Island—involved a PWR.

PWRs and BWRs share a number of important features. In both, the reactor core is enclosed in a heavy steel pressure vessel. To refuel the reactor, it must be shut down and the lid of the pressure vessel must be removed. Spent fuel rods are removed—a process that must be carried out under water because of the intense radioactivity—and replaced with fresh ones. Typically, a reactor is refueled about every 12–18 months, one-third of the fuel bundles being replaced. Refueling lasts 6–8 weeks, a time utilities seek to minimize because of the high cost of replacement power. The long time interval between refuelings has a positive aspect, though: It makes spent fuel from light-water reactors a less-than-ideal source of weapons-grade plutonium.

As we have seen, the use of a common moderator and coolant

is a safety feature of light-water reactors, a category that includes U.S. PWRs and BWRs. Loss of coolant means loss of moderator, which necessarily halts the fission chain reaction. The use of water as the moderator has an additional safety effect that occurs because the density of water decreases as its temperature rises: A slight increase in the reactor's power raises the water's temperature, lowering its density and therefore—since there are fewer hydrogen nuclei in a given volume—reducing the water's effectiveness as a moderator. As a result, fission slows and the temperature again drops. This feature of light-water reactors provides some stability and some protection against runaway chain reactions.

## Heavy-Water Reactors

Several countries, particularly Canada and Great Britain, have developed commercial power reactors moderated with heavy water. Since heavy water absorbs very few neutrons, these reactors can operate with unenriched uranium. The most popular HWR design is the CANDU (for Canadian Deuterium-Uranium). In the current generation of CANDU reactors, bundles of unenriched uranium fuel are mounted in individual coolant channels, through which pressurized heavy-water coolant circulates. The entire assembly of fuel bundles and coolant channels is immersed in a tank of unpressurized heavy water, which serves as the neutron moderator. Thus the CANDU design is cooled and moderated by heavy water, but with the two functions kept physically distinct. The pressurized coolant carries heat to steam generators, where it boils ordinary light water, which drives the turbine-generators as in a U.S. pressurized-water reactor.

Because the CANDU's coolant flows within individual pressurized channels, there is no need for the large, heavy pressure vessel found in U.S. light-water reactors. The lack of a single pressure vessel makes catastrophic failure of the high-pressure coolant system less likely than in a U.S. reactor. Furthermore, individual channels can be removed and refueled without shutting down the reactor. In practice, CANDU refueling is done almost continuously, with an average of fifteen fuel bundles replaced each day. Continuous refueling has several important implications. First, it makes controlling the reactor easier, because conditions within the reactor core remain essentially the same over time. (In contrast, the depletion of U-235 and the buildup of fission products over the long refueling interval make for substantial changes in the core of a U.S. light-water reactor.) As a result the CANDU design requires fewer control rods.

A second implication of continuous refueling entails the ever-present connection between nuclear power and nuclear weapons. Fuel that has spent a long time in a reactor—as happens in light-water reactors—is a poor source of bomb-grade plutonium. But in a reactor that can be refueled frequently, it is easier to "cook" fuel just long enough to optimize plutonium for use in nuclear weapons. With a continuously refueled reactor, it is also less practical for international inspection teams to monitor diversion of nuclear materials.

Which is safer, the American light-water design or the Canadian CANDU? In some of its design features, the CANDU has a safety edge over U.S. LWRs. And the CANDU avoids the need for uranium enrichment, a process that can be carried further to make bomb-grade uranium. On the other hand, the CANDU design shares with other continuously refueled reactors the ability to make bomb-grade plutonium, and its continuous refueling makes international inspection more difficult. In fact, a CANDU research reactor provided India with its first bomb plutonium. So which reactor is safer? That nuclear choice requires the weighing of complex considerations involving physics, engineering, and politics.

# CHAPTER 3

# Nuclear Accidents

# The Accident at Three Mile Island

## By the U.S. Nuclear Regulatory Commission

The worst nuclear power plant accident in U.S. history occurred at the Three Mile Island site in Pennsylvania on March 28, 1979. According to the following U.S. Nuclear Regulatory Commission fact sheet, the accident caused no deaths, injuries, or negative health effects. It did, however, lead to significant reforms in regulatory standards and emergency response procedures. The Nuclear Regulatory Commission (NRC), established by the Energy Reorganization Act of 1974, is an independent agency responsible for regulating the civilian use of nuclear materials. A tightening of commission standards was one of the many things that changed in light of the Three Mile Island accident.

The accident at the Three Mile Island Unit 2 (TMI-2) nuclear power plant near Middletown, Pennsylvania, on March 28, 1979, was the most serious in U.S. commercial nuclear power plant operating history, even though it led to no deaths or injuries to plant workers or members of the nearby community. But it brought about sweeping changes involving emergency response planning, reactor operator training, human factors, engineering, radiation protection, and many other areas of nuclear power plant operations. It also caused the U.S. Nuclear Regulatory Commission to tighten and heighten its regulatory oversight. Resultant changes in the nuclear power industry and at the NRC had the effect of enhancing safety.

The sequence of certain events—equipment malfunctions, design related problems and worker errors—led to a partial meltdown of the TMI-2 reactor core but only very small off-site releases of radioactivity.

U.S. Nuclear Regulatory Commission, *Fact Sheet: The Accident at Three Mile Island*. Washington, DC: Office of Public Affairs.

# The Leaking Valve

The accident began about 4:00 A.M. on March 28, 1979, when the plant experienced a failure in the secondary, non-nuclear section of the plant. The main feedwater pumps stopped running, caused by either a mechanical or electrical failure, which prevented the steam generators from removing heat. First the turbine, then the reactor automatically shut down. Immediately, the pressure in the primary system (the nuclear portion of the plant) began to increase. In order to prevent that pressure from becoming excessive, the pilot-operated relief valve (a valve located at the top of the pressurizer) opened. The valve should have closed when the pressure decreased by a certain amount, but it did not. Signals available to the operator failed to show that the valve was still open. As a result, cooling water poured out of the stuck-open valve and caused the core of the reactor to overheat.

As coolant flowed from the core through the pressurizer, the instruments available to reactor operators provided confusing information. There was no instrument that showed the level of coolant in the core. Instead, the operators judged the level of water in the core by the level in the pressurizer, and since it was high, they assumed that the core was properly covered with coolant. In addition, there was no clear signal that the pilot-operated relief valve was open. As a result, as alarms rang and warning lights flashed, the operators did not realize that the plant was experiencing a loss-of-coolant accident. They took a series of actions that made conditions worse by simply reducing the flow of coolant through the core.

Because adequate cooling was not available, the nuclear fuel overheated to the point at which the zirconium cladding (the long metal tubes which hold the nuclear fuel pellets) ruptured and the fuel pellets began to melt. It was later found that about one-half of the core melted during the early stages of the accident. Although the TMI-2 plant suffered a severe core meltdown, the most dangerous kind of nuclear power accident, it did not produce the worst-case consequences that reactor experts had long feared. In a worst-case accident, the melting of nuclear fuel would lead to a breach of the walls of the containment building and release massive quantities of radiation to the environment. But this did not occur as a result of the Three Mile Island accident.

The accident caught federal and state authorities off-guard. They were concerned about the small releases of radioactive gases that were measured off-site by the late morning of March 28 and even more concerned about the potential threat that the reactor posed to the surrounding population. They did not know that the core had melted, but they immediately took steps to try to gain control of the reactor and ensure adequate cooling to the core. The NRC's regional office in King of Prussia, Pennsylvania, was notified at 7:45 A.M. on March 28. By 8:00, NRC Headquarters in Washington, D.C., was alerted and the NRC Operations Center in Bethesda, Maryland, was activated. The regional office promptly dispatched the first team of inspectors to the site and other agencies, such as the Department of Energy and the Environmental Protection Agency, also mobilized their response teams. Helicopters hired by TMI's owner, General Public Utilities Nuclear, and the Department of Energy were sampling radioactivity in the atmosphere above the plant by midday. A team from the Brookhaven National Laboratory was also sent to assist in radiation monitoring. At 9:15 A.M., the White House was notified and at 11:00 A.M., all non-essential personnel were ordered off the plant's premises.

By the evening of March 28, the core appeared to be adequately cooled and the reactor appeared to be stable. But new concerns arose by the morning of Friday, March 30. A significant release of radiation from the plant's auxiliary building, performed to relieve pressure on the primary system and avoid curtailing the flow of coolant to the core, caused a great deal of confusion and consternation. In an atmosphere of growing uncertainty about the condition of the plant, the governor of Pennsylvania, Richard L. Thornburgh, consulted with the NRC about evacuating the population near the plant. Eventually, he and NRC Chairman Joseph Hendrie agreed that it would be prudent for those members of society most vulnerable to radiation to evacuate the area. Thornburgh announced that he was advising pregnant women and pre-school-age children within a 5-mile radius of the plant to leave the area.

Within a short time, the presence of a large hydrogen bubble in the dome of the pressure vessel, the container that holds the reactor core, stirred new worries. The concern was that the hydrogen bubble might burn or even explode and rupture the pressure vessel. In that event, the core would fall into the containment building and perhaps cause a breach of containment. The hydrogen bubble was a source of intense scrutiny and great anxiety, both among government authorities and the population, throughout the day on Saturday, March 31. The crisis ended when experts determined on Sunday, April 1, that the bubble could not burn or explode because of the absence of oxygen in the pressure vessel. Further, by that time, the utility had succeeded in greatly reducing the size of the bubble.

## Health Effects

Detailed studies of the radiological consequences of the accident have been conducted by the NRC, the Environmental Protection Agency, the Department of Health, Education and Welfare (now Health and Human Services), the Department of Energy, and the State of Pennsylvania. Several independent studies have also been conducted. Estimates are that the average dose to about 2 million people in the area was only about 1 millirem. To put this into context, exposure from a full set of chest x-rays is about 6 millirem. Compared to the natural radioactive background dose of about 100–125 millirem per year for the area, the collective dose to the community from the accident was very small. The maximum dose to a person at the site boundary would have been less than 100 millirem.

In the months following the accident, although questions were raised about possible adverse effects from radiation on human, animal, and plant life in the TMI area, none could be directly correlated to the accident. Thousands of environmental samples of air, water, milk, vegetation, soil, and foodstuffs were collected by various groups monitoring the area. Very low levels of radionuclides could be attributed to releases from the accident. However, comprehensive investigations and assessments by several well-respected organizations have concluded that in spite of serious damage to the reactor, most of the radiation was contained and that the actual release had negligible effects on the physical health of individuals or the environment.

## Impact of the Accident

The accident was caused by a combination of personnel error, design deficiencies, and component failures. There is no doubt that the accident at Three Mile Island permanently changed both the nuclear industry and the NRC. Public fear and distrust increased, NRC's regulations and oversight became broader and more robust, and management of the plants was scrutinized more carefully. The problems identified from careful analysis of the events during those days have led to permanent and sweeping changes in how NRC regulates its licensees—which, in turn, has reduced the risk to public health and safety.

Here are some of the major changes which have occurred since the accident:

- Upgrading and strengthening of plant design and equipment requirements. This includes fire protection, piping systems, auxiliary feedwater systems, containment building isolation, reliability of individual components (pressure relief valves and electrical circuit breakers), and the ability of plants to shut down automatically;
- Identifying human performance as a critical part of plant safety, revamping operator training and staffing requirements, followed by improved instrumentation and controls for operating the plant, and establishment of fitness-for-duty programs for plant workers to guard against alcohol or drug abuse;
- Improved instruction to avoid the confusing signals that plagued operations during the accident;
- Enhancement of emergency preparedness to include immediate NRC notification requirements for plant events and an NRC operations center which is now staffed 24 hours a day. Drills and response plans are now tested by licensees several times a year, and state and local agencies participate in drills with the Federal Emergency Management Agency and NRC;
- Establishment of a program to integrate NRC observations, findings, and conclusions about licensee performance and management effectiveness into a periodic, public report;
- Regular analysis of plant performance by senior NRC managers who identify those plants needing additional regulatory attention;
- Expansion of NRC's resident inspector program—first authorized in 1977—whereby at least two inspectors live nearby and work exclusively at each plant in the U.S to provide daily surveillance of licensee adherence to NRC regulations;
- Expansion of performance-oriented as well as safety-oriented inspections, and the use of risk assessment to identify vulnerabilities of any plant to severe accidents;
- Strengthening and reorganization of enforcement as a separate office within the NRC;

- The establishment of the Institute of Nuclear Power Operations (INPO), the industry's own "policing" group, and formation of what is now the Nuclear Energy Institute to provide a unified industry approach to generic nuclear regulatory issues, and interaction with NRC and other government agencies;
- The installing of additional equipment by licensees to mitigate accident conditions, and monitor radiation levels and plant status;
- Employment of major initiatives by licensees in early identification of important safety-related problems, and in collecting and assessing relevant data so lessons of experience can be shared and quickly acted upon;
- Expansion of NRC's international activities to share enhanced knowledge of nuclear safety with other countries in a number of important technical areas.

## Current Status

Today, the TMI-2 reactor is permanently shut down and defueled, with the reactor coolant system drained, the radioactive water decontaminated and evaporated, radioactive waste shipped off-site to an appropropriate disposal site, reactor fuel and core debris shipped off-site to a Department of Energy facility, and the remainder of the site being monitored. The owner says it will keep the facility in long-term, monitored storage until the operating license for the TMI-1 plant expires at which time both plants will be decommissioned.

# What Went Wrong at Three Mile Island

## By James R. Chiles

In his book, *Inviting Disaster*, technology writer James R. Chiles discusses his concept of technological blind spots—the unseen or poorly understood parts of complex machines that often bring about malfunction or disasters. In this selection, Chiles describes the blind spots at the root of the worst nuclear power plant accident in United States history: the partial reactor meltdown at the Three Mile Island plant in Pennsylvania. Chiles cites faulty control readings, inadequate training and narrow thinking on the part of operators, and a bad valve as contributing factors in a near-disaster that might have been averted if these "blind spots" had been foreseen and remedied.

The most expensive blind spot in history happened on March 28, 1979, at the power plant called Three Mile Island Unit 2, near Harrisburg, Pennsylvania. Though the plant looked fine on the outside after the crisis was over, on the inside the reactor core was a complete wreck. Half the fuel in the reactor vessel had melted, and most of the rest had tumbled into a heap of rubble on top of that. Still, the thick-walled stainless steel reactor vessel held the fuel from breaking out the bottom, just long enough.

The President's Commission on Three Mile Island concluded that the reactor core came within a half hour of total meltdown. Notwithstanding the media's excitement over the "hydrogen bubble" [building up inside the reactor] after the first day, it's clear now that the first three hours at TMI-2 were the most critical. While it's possible that the reactor core could have melted into the

James R. Chiles, *Inviting Disaster: Lessons from the Edge of Technology: An Inside Look at Catastrophes and Why They Happen*. New York: HarperCollins, 2001. Copyright © 2001 by James R. Chiles. All rights reserved. Reproduced by permission of the publisher.

ground in the so-called China Syndrome, it's equally likely that fuel melting out the bottom of the reactor vessel would have set off a mighty steam explosion when it hit the pool of water in the bottom of the thick concrete containment building, breaking open the building to release a massive cloud of radioactive steam across the towns and farms of southern Pennsylvania. Though news media excitement peaked a few days later, the worst danger had passed on the same day it started and certainly was over by April 1, when President Jimmy Carter arrived at Harrisburg, Pennsylvania, to reassure the public. According to Walter Mondale, during the visit a woman spoke up after Carter said that the danger was over. "I believe you," she said, "because if there was any danger the vice president would be here instead.". . .

Three Mile Island Unit 2 cost General Public Utilities and the rest of us more than $4 billion, making it the nation's worst industrial disaster in cash terms. It was so big that two decades later, lawyers are still fighting over who should pick up the cost. . . .

## Following the Heat

Just as journalism-school students learn to follow the money, it helps to follow the heat in understanding the layout of TMI-2 (see Figure 1). We can think of TMI as three sets of pipes linked together like loops of a chain, working together to move heat from the reactor core to the outside world, taking it through generators along the way that harnessed the heat and turned it into electric power. We'll call the first set of piping the "reactor coolant" pipes. The reactor coolant pipes took high temperature, high pressure water to extract heat from the one hundred tons of hot uranium in the reactor core. The reactor coolant pipes were entirely inside the containment dome, out of view. Traveling inside these pipes, highly pressurized water extracted heat from the reactor pressure vessel and carried it off to a heat exchanger. Inside the heat exchanger, what we'll call the "steam-making pipes" accepted the handoff of heat and carried it from the containment building. Inside the steam-making pipes, ultrapure water flashed into steam. Arriving at the turbine building, the steam passed through a set of turbines and generators, making 880 megawatts of electricity to sell.

Then a third set of pipes, which we'll call the "external cooling" pipes, conducted the waste heat away from the steam-making pipes and carried it outside the turbine building to the top of giant

# Figure 1: Three Mile Island Unit 2

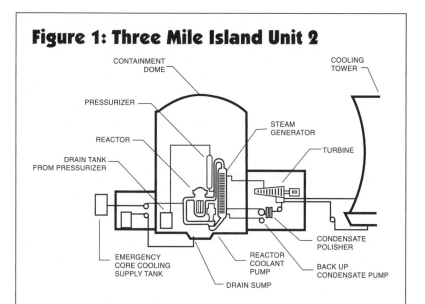

## Probable Sequence

1. Malfunction during maintenance work causes condensate valves to close.
2. Reactor coolant heats up and pressure rises; pilot operated relief valve (PORV) on pressurizer opens.
3. PORV does not close on automatic command.
4. Coolant begins draining out of reactor through pressurizer.
5. Operators cut back on emergency cooling system and drain more coolant, thinking reactor coolant level is dangerously high.
6. Problem is discovered after half of reactor core melts.

Adapted from Senate Committee on Environment and Public Works.

concrete cooling towers. As the hot water trickled down the inside of the towers, some of it evaporated, and in doing so it cooled the water that remained; pumps sent the cooled water back through the external cooling pipes, back into the turbine building to remove more heat. Of the three piping loops, the external cooling pipes were the most visible and accessible to people working at Three Mile Island; even nearby residents could see when that part of the system was operating to bring heat out of the plant, because of the plumes of condensed water vapor that the cooling towers gave off.

The operators and maintenance people were less in sync with

the steam-making pipes, since those pipes carried high-pressure steam and very hot water and were not accessible where they passed through the containment building. But the maintenance people could see and even touch this set of pipes where they passed through the turbine building. And by closing isolation valves they could even separate out some of the steam-making pipes from the rest of the system and work on them while the reactor was operating.

Both these loops of piping were visible to the human eye and open to the wrench, then, in their own ways. Not so the third, the reactor coolant pipes, which held the hottest, most radioactive water. These were entirely out of sight from operators and maintenance workers, buried deep inside the containment building. These pipes and vessels could not be worked on while the reactor was operating, since the pressure, radioactivity, and heat would have made the work unsafe. Not even cameras revealed what the reactor coolant pipes would be doing in an emergency.

Yet all three links of this chain were equally important. The analogy works because a chain is only as strong as its weakest link; at TMI-2, all three loops had to work if the reactor was to stay within its temperature limits. If any of the three loops of piping failed, the reactor would go into an emergency condition, relying solely on short-term supplies of cooling water. The emergency could happen even after a reactor shutdown, after control rods had stopped the critical mass of full-power fission. For hours after a shutdown, the one-hundred-ton reactor core kept producing so much decay heat that the thermal energy could not safely remain inside the pressure vessel without some kind of cooling.

## March 28, 1979

In the early hours of March 28, 1979, the situation on Three Mile Island was as follows. The Unit 1 power plant was down for repairs and testing; Unit 2 was running at 3 million horsepower, enough to supply a city of five hundred thousand people. Big systems like this always have at least a few things out of whack, or maybe more than a few. Down in the hot and cavernous basement of the turbine building at Unit 2, Don Miller and Harold Farst had opened up a part of the steam-making loop for maintenance. It may seem to you like an odd time to do maintenance, but the system had valves to isolate this area from the high pressures and temperatures of the rest of the steam-making pipes.

The problem concerned one of the giant water filters (called a "condensate polisher") in the steam-making loop. All night the men had been trying to shake loose tons of tiny plastic beads in one of the demineralizer tanks. The beads, with the consistency of coarse sand, had jammed into a pipe leading out of filter tank number 7. The bead-jamming problem had plagued the operators on and off for months; before it had always yielded to blasts of compressed air through a pipe stuck in from underneath. Miller had been trying this for hours, to no avail. The problem was not critical; there were seven other filtering tanks to handle the five thousand gallons of water needed every minute at the steam generator. The reactor was running at 97 percent full power.

At some point during the frustrating hours of fooling around with the compressed air jet and the filter tank, a few ounces of water seeped backward into the compressed air lines, undetected by those on the scene. It took a little while for the water to snake its way into the instruments that relied on compressed air, but then things happened quickly. At 36 seconds past 4:00 A.M., the leaking water from the polisher repair attempt reached the control line to the big valves controlling all the condensate polishers. The automatic controls interpreted this tiny bit of water in their air lines as a deviation from proper conditions and so shut all the valves that let coolant through. This acted like an instant roadblock in the steam-making pipes. The inertia of five thousand gallons of water a minute, stopping so quickly, tore one of the big pipes loose in the turbine building, pulled out controls, and sprayed the place with scalding water. Without water, pumps downstream cut off, so steam stopped flowing from the heat exchanger in the containment building; that made the generating turbines shut down, too.

## Playing Its Last Song

In 1893, Rudyard Kipling published a poem called "M'Andrew's Hymn," which called for a poet to sing the "Song o' Steam." Three Mile Island sang its own song: every month or so, over the single year from its first operation, escape pipes had howled like an enormous whistle as valves inside the turbine building opened to dump excess steam. That morning, the reactor played its last song as the turbines shut down. For at least a mile in every direction, anyone awake in the Middletown, Pennsylvania, area could hear the sound of a million pounds of high-pressure steam, shrieking into the sky. It woke up one woman a quarter mile away.

So it happened that the three-link chain of cooling pipes suffered a broken link. With the steam-making pipes shut off, the water in the reactor coolant loop had no place to dump its heat. Following automatic "scram" commands from a computer, cadmium control rods plummeted into the reactor, ending the nuclear chain reaction and cutting back heat production at the core to a few percent of full power. Still the temperature rose and the water began expanding, as things will do when heated. The expanding water made the pressure climb from the usual value of 2,150 pounds per square inch.

The reactor coolant loop had only one open space for the water to expand into. It was called the pressurizer tank, and it was forty-two feet high, located inside the containment building along with the rest of the coolant piping. The pressurizer tank acted like a shock absorber to the reactor coolant piping. On an ordinary day the tank was supposed to be about half filled with reactor coolant water at the bottom, leaving steam as a cushion in the upper part. Automatic controls maintained the right balance of water and steam by either cooling or heating the contents of the pressurizer tank.

At the very top of the pressurizer was a safety valve to let off steam if pressure rose too fast for the automatic controls. Deep inside the containment building, the pilot operated relief valve (PORV) opened as intended, reducing pressure by letting steam out the top of the pressurizer when the water level rose. That sent a mix of water and steam down a drainpipe to a storage tank on the floor of the containment building.

There were many problems at Three Mile Island Unit 2 that morning, but the PORV was the one that reduced the reactor core to slag and rubble. When the pressure stabilized a few seconds later and the electronic command came to close the PORV, the valve stuck open instead. That left a hole about the diameter of a Ping-Pong ball in the reactor coolant system. It wasn't discovered until more than two hours later. . . .

## Inside the Control Room

Come inside the beige-paneled control room at TMI-2, eight seconds after the valves slammed shut and blocked off the steam-making pipes. The intense investigation into TMI gave us the best record, ever, of how things look to the people trapped inside the fast-moving, scary world of a major system failure. Like Alice inside the rabbit hole, the operators did their best to impose order onto seeming chaos. And they might have succeeded had they been able to see what was really happening inside the containment building only a few dozen yards away.

TMI-2 had four Nuclear Regulatory Commission-licensed reactor operators on the 11:00 P.M. to 7:00 A.M. shift, plus extra men to work on machinery maintenance. The licensed men in the control room at 4:00 A.M. were shift supervisor Bill Zewe and two operators, Craig Faust and Ed Frederick. The shift foreman, Fred Schiemann, was still down in the basement of the turbine building with Don Miller and his partner, trying to fix the condensate polishers.

A two-tone control room warning horn went off shortly after 4:00 A.M., and Faust saw lights warning him that pumps in the steam-making pipes had shut down. Zewe came out of his glass-walled office to join the others at the panel. It showed that three emergency pumps were coming on-line automatically, to keep water moving along in the steam-making pipes and thus assist the flow of heat out of the reactor.

Pressure was going up in the reactor coolant loop; that was to be expected at this point, because of all the heat trapped by the blockage in the steam-making pipes. A bright red glowing light showed that an electric signal had ordered the PORV to open and vent any pressure over 2,255 pounds per square inch. Shortly afterward the pressure dropped and the PORV light went out. Operators thought this meant that the PORV had closed, but all it really meant was that the command had been sent to close it. Nothing showed them that the valve had actually stuck open. The false PORV light was the first deceptive control reading that morning, but not the last.

During the first minute, the level of water showing in the pressurizer tank was dropping, too; also to be expected as the reactor heat dropped and the water cooled. Working from his books of emergency procedures, Frederick turned on high-pressure pumps to throw some extra water into the reactor coolant pipes. This would replace some of the volume lost as the coolant water shrank. The pressurizer water level began to creep upward from its low point of 158 inches. That gauge showed the water level compared to the length of the pressurizer tank, which was a vertical tube. The highest possible reading on the gauge was four hundred inches. Schiemann arrived, having run up eight flights of stairs from the turbine building basement. Schiemann took a seat at a panel on the left side of the console, where he could watch the water level in the pressurizer.

The rising water should have stopped but didn't. When it hit three hundred inches at four minutes into the crisis, Frederick cut back on the water injection pumps, but the water level still went up even though pressure was dropping. TMI-2 was now cruising somewhere outside the operators' familiar world. Past four hundred inches on the gauge, the operators knew, there would be nowhere for rising water volume to go.

Think of filling a closed set of metal pipes with water, right to the top, leaving no air space at all, then sealing them up tight. Reactor operators call that condition "going solid." If you heated those filled pipes just a little more, the increasing water volume would create so much pressure that the pipe would have to burst. In a reactor the coolant water would turn to steam, and the voids left in the pipes would let the core overheat. It would be the much-feared "loss of coolant accident." Said the TMI operating manual in unusually clear words for a technical manual, the pressurizer "must not be filled with coolant to solid conditions (400 inches) at any time except as required for system hydrostatic tests.". . .

## Sticking with a Theory

The TMI operators stuck with their theory that the reactor was going solid. Maybe a pump or valve somewhere had gotten stuck and was forcing more water in, defying all commands. If cold water was coming in, that might explain why the pressure was dropping. It was hard to concentrate, with the main alarm Klaxon going and more than a hundred alarm lights flashing. So the operators began letting water out of the primary coolant piping at the rate of 160 gallons a minute.

Finally, having cut off the inflow of nearly all emergency cooling water, and having opened a valve to let more water out, at 4:06 A.M. the operators saw the water level stop climbing as it reached the top of the gauge. It looked like a hairsbreadth escape from the do-not-exceed point of four hundred inches. For the next two hours, the water level gauge would hold the operators' attention like a cobra in a basket. It would drift down when they let more water out of the primary system; then it would creep back up toward four hundred inches. It was so strange that Zewe sent his assistants to cross-check the other instruments, to see whether the water level gauge was showing bad information. The word came back later that the gauge was correct.

Other workers and managers on the graveyard shift began to gather, consulting in low tones and offering to watch panels under Zewe's direction. The control room had only a single phone line to the outside world. Even the computer was far away: although the computer was capable of recording key information about hundreds of alarms as fast as they came in, it could only print out fifteen lines of information per minute. The printer fell more than two hours behind at one point in the emergency.

By 4:20 A.M., the combination of choked-down emergency pumps and coolant water flowing out the letdown valve seemed to be working well enough because the pressurizer water level was hovering somewhere around 370 inches. So Zewe left the control room to see if he could straighten out the mess at the condensate polishers. But when Zewe got back at about 5:00 A.M., affairs had taken a very serious and unexpected turn. The four giant pumps in the containment building that forced water through the reactor coolant pipes were shaking themselves to pieces as the pump impellers met cavities of steam, sped up, then slammed into solid water and slowed down.

Pumps and fittings could not survive this abuse without cracking. Worse, this didn't fit at all with the operators' prevailing theory that the primary system was nearly full of water. Instead it was a strong signal that the water was full of steam, meaning that the water level might be dropping below the top of the reactor core. Following standard procedures once again, at 5:14 A.M. the operators shut off two of the pumps, and the last two a half hour later.

## Calling for Help

It was about 5:00 A.M., when the four reactor coolant pumps began shaking, that an engineer used the precious single phone line from the control room to call Brian Mehler at his home in Palmyra, Pennsylvania. They needed him as backup and wanted him to come as soon as possible. Mehler was not assigned to Unit 2 at the time; the duty roster for the day showed Mehler coming in at 7:00 A.M. to work as a shift supervisor at Unit 1. Mehler had been working over at Unit 2 the day before, and someone must have thought he might have an opinion as to what was going wrong. . . .

Fifteen minutes after arriving at the control room, Mehler had two theories in mind. One explanation could be a blown circuit breaker that had knocked out the electric heaters in the pressurizer tank. These heaters were supposed to come on if pressure dropped, making more steam at the top of the pressurizer. Mehler figured that if the heaters weren't working, the system would have trouble keeping the water level down where it was supposed to be. Mehler sent a man to check on the breaker panel.

Without waiting for an answer about the circuit breakers, Mehler turned to the other possible explanation, a fairly small leak somewhere in the reactor coolant system, and one that had opened very early in the sequence. . . .

Mehler asked the supervisors in charge if they minded if he went ahead and closed an electrically operated valve that would isolate the pressurizer tank from the PORV. . . .

At the time Mehler got his clearance to proceed, the system pressure had dropped to nine hundred pounds per square inch. He leaned over to Fred Schiemann and asked him to close the block valve. Within seconds, a gauge in the control room relayed news about the first good thing to happen on Three Mile Island in the last two hours and eighteen minutes. The primary coolant pressure was heading back up.

Core damage was well under way by then and would continue for much of the day; and it would be eleven hours more before the operators brought the water level up enough to cover the core, but TMI's worst overheating had been stopped less than an hour from disaster. . . .

The primary system had lost about two-thirds of its coolant, allowing half the core to melt; perhaps twenty tons of uranium had melted into a slag pool at the bottom of the reactor vessel. The first direct sign of how serious the damage was became apparent the next day when a water sample was taken. It was loaded with black grit and radioactive particles from the ruptured fuel rods. The full story of the first day's chaos in the containment building would take fourteen years and a billion dollars to sort out completely.

# The Chernobyl Accident

## By Robert Peter Gale and Thomas Hauser

The 1986 nuclear power plant explosion at Chernobyl (then part of the Soviet Union, now Ukraine) was by far the worst such accident in history. The following is a brief description of the events that occurred on April 25 and 26 of that year. This selection comes from the memoir of Robert Peter Gale, an American physician who traveled to the Soviet Union in Chernobyl's aftermath to help treat radiation victims. Gale's coauthor, Thomas Hauser, is an attorney, sportswriter, and novelist who has written, among other things, a highly acclaimed biography of boxer Muhammad Ali.

**D**uring World War II, the United States and Germany were not alone in considering the potential of atomic weapons. As early as 1939, Russian physicists had recognized the possibility of harnessing a nuclear chain reaction. Three years later, [Soviet leader] Joseph Stalin ordered that high priority be given to investigating the military applications of nuclear fission, and in 1949 the Soviets successfully detonated an atomic explosion. Nuclear parity between the superpowers followed, and thereafter the Soviet government moved to implement an energy policy based in significant part on nuclear fission. By 1984, 10 percent of all electricity generated in the Soviet Union came from nuclear sources, and officials were targeting a 50 percent figure for the year 2000.

The pride of the Soviet nuclear program was a planned six-unit complex at Chernobyl. Chernobyl Unit Number 1 went into service in 1977, and was followed by Units 2, 3, and 4 in 1978, 1981, and 1983 respectively. Units 5 and 6 were scheduled to come on line in 1988. The Chernobyl reactors were similar to one another

Dr. Robert Peter Gale and Thomas Hauser, *Final Warning: The Legacy of Chernobyl*. New York: Warner Books, 1988. Copyright © 1988 by Robert Peter Gale. All rights reserved. Reproduced by permission of the publisher.

in design, but differed from units in the United States in two significant respects. First, rather than using water as a moderator, the Chernobyl units employed graphite. And as a consequence of this and several other design features, chain reactions within the reactor were more likely to run out of control in the event of a loss-of-coolant accident. And second, while the Chernobyl units were protected by strong walls, they were housed in buildings which lacked reinforced concrete domes typical of Western containment structures. Whether either of these factors contributed to the scope of the disaster which ultimately occurred is subject to dispute, given the magnitude of the Chernobyl explosion.

## Two Blasts, Three Seconds Apart

The chain of events leading to disaster began on the morning of April 25, 1986. Unit Number 4 was scheduled to be taken out of service for routine maintenance, and the plant's electrical engineers wanted to conduct a test to determine how long the turbine-generators would continue to produce electricity to run the water pumps necessary to cool the reactor after the normal electrical supply had been interrupted.

At one A.M., the reactor's power level was lowered to prepare for the test. Then, over the next twenty-four hours, technicians systematically disconnected power regulation and emergency cooling systems which would have automatically shut the reactor down and interfered with the test. Finally, at 1:23 on the morning of April 26, 1986—twenty-four hours after preparation for the test had begun—the flow of steam to the turbine was halted. Almost immediately, the cooling pumps slowed, diminishing the flow of cooling water to the reactor core. Normally, at this point, the reactor would have shut down, but the automatic shutdown system was one of six safety mechanisms that had been deliberately disconnected. Within seconds, there was a massive heat buildup in the reactor core, triggering an uncontrolled chain reaction. Power surged. At 1:23 A.M., the Unit Number 4 reactor exploded.

There were two blasts, three seconds apart. The first was caused by steam, the second by steam or hydrogen which had formed when the fuel-rod cladding began to melt and interacted with water in the pressure vessel. The reactor core was torn apart. Its thousand-ton cover-plate was propelled upward, causing the building roof above the reactor to collapse. A deadly plume of radioactive material—more than was released at Hiroshima and Nagasaki [where the first atomic bombs were dropped]—shot into the air, forming a fiery image above the roof before dispersing into the atmosphere. Exposed to intense heat and open air, the graphite moderator began to burn. Radioactive water gushed into the reactor hall. Hot chunks of fuel and metal landed on what was left of the building roof and the roofs of adjacent buildings. Thirty fires began to burn.

Within minutes, the nuclear plant's firefighting unit was on the scene—twenty-eight men under the command of Major Leonid Telyatnikov. "You had the impression you could see the radiation," Telyatnikov said later. "There were flashes of light springing from place to place, substances glowing, luminescent, a bit like sparklers."

Telyatnikov ordered a "stage three" alarm, the highest for Soviet firefighters, summoning 250 reserves from as far away as Kiev. Then he and the few men available began working desperately to halt the fires. Their primary concern was that Unit Number 4 shared a ventilation system with, and was housed in the same reactor hall as, Unit Number 3. If the fire spread and Unit 3 went up in flames, the disaster would double in magnitude.

A dozen firemen in the Unit 3 reactor block attacked the blaze with hand-held extinguishers. As that struggle progressed, Telyatnikov led six men up a hundred-foot ladder to the collapsed roof of the reactor hall. Because of the heat, what was left of the asphalt roof had begun to melt. With each step, the firemen's boots sunk into the bitumen, and they had to strain to pull free. Poisonous fumes made breathing difficult; visibility was near zero. Water that was poured on the flames turned instantly to scalding radioactive steam.

Firefighting units from nearby towns began to arrive at three-thirty A.M. Still, the fires raged. "We knew about the radiation," Telyatnikov said later. "We were trying to get the fire before the radiation got us. We are firemen. This is what we were trained for. We are supposed to fight fires. We knew we must stay to the end. That was our duty."

Shortly before dawn, all fires except one in the Unit 4 reactor core (which would burn for weeks) had been extinguished. The reactor hall was in shambles. Of the seven men who fought the blaze on the building roof, all but Telyatnikov (who was hospitalized for three months) would die as a result of radiation exposure.

# Chernobyl, Ten Years Later

## By Neely Tucker

In 1996 on the tenth anniversary of the Chernobyl accident, scientists, health care professionals, and others gathered at a symposium in Vienna, Austria, to discuss its consequences. As this news article shows, opinions differed on whether the primary outcomes were "mass hysteria" and stress or more fundamental health disorders such as thyroid cancer, breast cancer, and leukemia. The article's author, Neely Tucker, worked as a foreign correspondent for many years, first in Europe, then Zimbabwe. He now works for the *Washington Post*.

Ten years ago this month, the No. 4 reactor at the Chernobyl nuclear power station in the Ukraine exploded, showering much of Eastern Europe with 200 times more radiation than Hiroshima and Nagasaki absorbed from the atomic bombs dropped during World War II.

Now, a decade after the April 26, 1986, disaster exposed 5 million people to increased doses of radiation, scientists said Wednesday they are still unsure of the true extent of Chernobyl-related diseases.

"Fifty more years are needed to really know the effect of Chernobyl," said University of New Mexico Professor Fred Mettler, who led an international health assessment team to the site in northeastern Ukraine in 1990.

## Mass Hysteria, Stress, and Cancer

With hard facts scarce, a panel of international experts said Wednesday the fear created by the accident at Chernobyl has led to "mass hysteria" in Ukraine and the neighboring nation of Belarus. This hysteria has wreaked far more damage to people's health in those areas than the radiation itself.

Speaking at a symposium on the 10th anniversary of the world's worst nuclear accident, health-care professionals, scientists and sociologists portrayed the explosion at Chernobyl's No. 4 reactor as an ecological disaster that has bred hysteria, malaise and a caustic fatalism in Ukraine, Belarus and affected areas of western Russia.

Those worries have, in turn, set off a chain reaction of stress-related illnesses that are far worse than the actual radiation sickness or disease so far caused by excessive radiation, the panel members said.

The four-day, 700-delegate conference, which ends Friday, is sponsored by the European Commission, the International Atomic Energy Agency and the World Health Organization.

"Depression, excessive smoking, high blood pressure, stomach ulcers, alcoholism, headaches and constant fatigue are the most health problems found," said Terence Lee, a psychologist from the University of St. Andrews, Scotland, who has studied the Chernobyl accident for a decade.

"The widespread demoralization and poor health in these areas must be attributed to stress, not radiation," said Lee in a conclusion hotly debated by Ukrainian government officials.

The only health problem directly attributable to radiation is thyroid cancer in children, the panel said, summing up a decade of research. Rates of thyroid cancer in children who were under the age of 14 at the time of the accident are up 200 percent, the WHO reported, but the total number of children affected is still less than 1,000, and fatalities are rare.

Expected jumps in leukemia rates have so far failed to surface, the research showed, but are likely to increase over 10 to 20 years. For example, cancer rates in Hiroshima and Nagasaki, Japanese cities hit with atomic bombs by the United States in World War II, only began to increase 10 years after the U.S. bombing raids of 1945.

"Many cancers don't show up for years," said Mettler, who is chairman of New Mexico's Department of Radiology. "For example, with breast cancer, if a young girl was radiated, you probably won't see the cancer show up until she is about 50."

Compounding the assessment problem is that reliable data is hard to come by in impoverished Ukraine, Belarus and western Russia. Few hospitals have computers or share data, especially across international lines. Records "are often kept in a dusty note-book somewhere on top of a filing cabinet and are highly unreli-able," said Lee.

Fearing a western propaganda coup, leaders of the former So-viet Union ordered doctors to falsify records and destroy data shortly after the accident to hide its full effects, many Soviet doc-tors have said.

## Evacuations

At least 135,000 people were evacuated from an 18-mile radius around the damaged reactor shortly after the accident. Another 100,000 were moved over the next four years. The wetlands of Be-larus, a nation where one-fifth of the 10 million people still live on contaminated land, have aggravated the situation by absorbing the radiation from Chernobyl and spreading it across the country in groundwater.

Today, only 640 people live within the main exclusions zones around Chernobyl in Ukraine. The 6,000 workers operating the remaining two reactors at Chernobyl are taken by shuttle trains some 30 miles away to a new city built just for them.

The 50,000 people of Pripyat, the town originally built for plant workers, were evacuated within 48 hours of the 1986 accident. To-day in Pripyat, coffee cups still sit on tables, pictures hang on some apartment walls and rotted linen still covers a few tables in an abandoned restaurant.

Despite the army of experts who have visited Chernobyl since the disaster, the health effects of the accident are still fiercely de-bated by advocates and opponents of nuclear energy. A recent atomic energy conference in Minsk, Belarus, concluded that only 45 deaths were attributable to the accident. The Ukrainian Health Ministry says the figure is more than 100,000 in that country alone.

Given the disparity, the long legacy of Soviet repression of in-formation and the desire by western nations to shut down Cher-nobyl, people in the region believe the worst.

Lee, the Scottish sociologist, presented a study Wednesday that showed 45 percent of people living in contaminated areas thought they had an illness related to Chernobyl. The figure for clean, radiation-free zones nearby was still 30 percent. He called the be-lief hysteria and attributed it to "stress caused by ignorance and irresponsible reporting by the media."

But the view of Chernobyl as primarily a psychosomatic disor-
der rankled some at the conference, and will be greeted with dis-
belief in Ukraine, Belarus and western Russia.

"Five years ago, the IAEA [International Atomic Energy
Agency] said there were no health problems due to Chernobyl, just
fears of it," said Nuala Ahern, a European Parliament member rep-
resenting Ireland. "Now thyroid cancer has emerged and they've
very reluctantly admitted that. So I'm skeptical of what I'm hearing today. . . . I think there are going to be far worse problems that
become apparent over time."

# Evidence Linking Radiation from Chernobyl to Thyroid Cancer

**By Kristen Woodward**

Scientists, doctors, and observers seem to agree that the population of Chernobyl, Ukraine, has experienced increased incidence of thyroid cancer since the nuclear reactor there exploded. The following selection describes a recent study conducted at the Fred Hutchinson Cancer Research Center on the relationship between the level of radiation exposure (the dose) and incidence of thyroid cancer in Chernobyl's citizens. The Fred Hutchinson Cancer Research Center is dedicated to research to help understand, treat, and prevent cancer and other life-threatening illnesses. It was founded by Dr. William Hutchinson whose brother Fred was a major league baseball player and died of lung cancer at the age of forty-five. The selection's author, Kristen Woodward, works in media relations at the center.

The risk of thyroid cancer rises with increasing radiation dose, according to the most thorough risk analysis for thyroid cancer to date among people who grew up in the shadow of the 1986 Chernobyl power-plant disaster.

The incidence of thyroid cancer was 45 times greater among those who received the highest radiation dose as compared to those in the lowest-dose group, according to a team of American and Russian researchers led by Scott Davis, Ph.D., and colleagues at Fred Hutchinson Cancer Research Center. They report their findings in the September [2004] issue of *Radiation Research.*

"This is the first study of its kind to establish a dose-response relationship between radiation dose from Chernobyl and thyroid cancer," said Davis, referring to the observation that as radiation doses increase, so does the risk of thyroid cancer. "We found a significant increased risk of thyroid cancer among people exposed as children to radiation from Chernobyl, and that the risk increased as a function of radiation dose." Having such information in hand, Davis said, may help officials better predict what long-term health effects to expect in the event of a similar nuclear accident or terrorist attack.

## The Cancer Burden

"Another potential benefit of the findings is that it allows officials to more accurately understand and document the magnitude of the thyroid-cancer burden that has resulted from Chernobyl. This information will be important in designing and maintaining programs targeted toward the victims of the disaster."

While about 30 people were killed immediately from the blast, which remains the worst accident of its kind in history, an estimated 5 million people were exposed to the resulting radiation.

"Prior to Chernobyl, thyroid cancer in children was practically nonexistent. Today we see dozens and dozens of cases a year in the regions contaminated by the disaster, and the incidence continues to rise," Davis said. "This provides some evidence that there's an excess of thyroid cancer in children and in people who were children at the time of the accident. However until now nobody had taken the next step to find out just how much a risk there is and whether it rises along with radiation dose."

While previous Chernobyl studies have relied on broadstroke estimates of radiation exposure based on such factors as ground contamination, geographic proximity to the northern Ukraine plant or other surrogate measures of exposure, this study is the first of its kind to factor into the equation individualized estimates of radiation dose based on in-person interviews about diet and other lifestyle factors, said Davis, a member of Fred Hutchinson's Public Health Sciences Division.

"After all these years, many efforts have been made by various research groups around the world to study the health effects of Chernobyl, and hundreds of scientific papers have been published.

But ours is the first report that provides quantitative estimates of thyroid-cancer risk in relation to individual estimates of radiation dose," said Davis, also chairman of the Department of Epidemiology at the University of Washington School of Public Health and Community Medicine in Seattle. . . .

## The Research Team and Its Task

The Fred Hutchinson team organized a collaborative effort with a dozen scientists at four Russian institutions to conduct this research: the Medical Radiological Research Center (in Obninsk), the Bryansk Diagnostic Center and the Bryansk Institute of Pathology (both in Bryansk), and the National Center of Hematology (in Moscow). All investigators were members of the International Consortium for Research on the Health Effects of Radiation funded by the U.S. Office of Naval Research. The researchers focused their efforts on the western part of the Bryansk Oblast of Russia. This region, located about 66 miles northeast of Chernobyl, is the most heavily contaminated area in the Russian Federation. This was the first study of this type among residents of the Russian Federation exposed to Chernobyl radiation.

Working through a local cancer registry, the researchers identified 26 people with thyroid cancer who were less than 20 years old when the Chernobyl accident occurred; the majority were under 16 when their thyroid cancers were diagnosed. They then identified 52 healthy control subjects from the general population for comparison purposes. The controls and cancer cases were matched by age and place of residence at the time of the accident.

The researchers then set about collecting information from these individuals and their mothers or fathers that would allow them to estimate each person's radiation dose using computer models. Interviews took place in the home and were conducted by Russian physicians.

## Sources of Poisoning

Individual doses depended largely on the ingestion patterns of food contaminated with radioactive iodine-131 (I-131), which concentrates in the thyroid gland. The primary source of food-based I-131 was milk from cows that grazed on contaminated pastures. Radiation doses to the thyroid increased along with the amount of milk and dairy products consumed.

External, airborne radiation and contamination of other foods also contributed somewhat to the overall dose, depending on the person's proximity to the plant at the time of the accident. These doses were all received within the first few months after the accident, before the I-131 in the environment decayed into non-radioactive elements. While other radioactive contaminants remain in the area, they do not cause appreciable doses of radiation to the thyroid.

In addition to the study's ability to estimate individual radiation doses based on personal interviews, other strengths of the study included the fact that all cases of thyroid cancer were confirmed independently by a panel of expert pathologists, and the study focused on people exposed as young children and adolescents, a group that is likely to be most susceptible to the effects of radiation exposure to the thyroid gland. Limitations of the study included its small sample size and its reliance on individual recall for reporting factors such as milk-consumption patterns that were used to estimate radiation dose.

## Broadening the Study

Efforts are under way to investigate a larger population in a similar fashion to see if these findings can be replicated, Davis said. For his contributions to the field, earlier this year Davis became the first foreign epidemiologist elected to the Russian Academy of Medical Sciences.

The group's status in that country is on a par with the esteemed National Academy of Sciences in the United States. In May he received an honorary diploma in Moscow.

Davis and colleagues have extended their cancer-risk studies to older Chernobyl survivors and are investigating how the damage caused to DNA by radiation influences the risk of developing thyroid cancer.

This work is part of Fred Hutchinson's Global Health Initiative, which focuses on international collaboration to understand and solve some of the most widespread health problems in the world, including cancer and infectious diseases.

# More Nuclear Reactor Accidents Are Likely

**By David Lochbaum**

In the following article, nuclear safety engineer David Lochbaum likens the probability of a nuclear power plant accident to the probability of getting a row of matching pictures in a slot machine. According to him, if three events—an initiating event, failure of backup equipment, and worker error—occur simultaneously, an accident may occur. David Lochbaum works for and published this viewpoint with the Union of Concerned Scientists, an organization that was founded in 1969 by a group of Massachusetts Institute of Technology professors and students who were concerned about the misuse of science and technology.

On March 28, 1979, the reactor core at the Three Mile Island Unit 2 facility outside Harrisburg, Pennsylvania, suffered a partial meltdown when a minor plant incident was complicated by equipment failures and personnel errors. According to surveys conducted by the Pennsylvania Department of Health, approximately 144,000 people living within 15 miles of the plant evacuated the area during the crisis. Nearby schools were closed for a week after the accident. Lethal levels of radiation prevented plant workers from entering the reactor containment building for nearly a year. The severely damaged facility never resumed operating and cost several hundred million dollars to clean up.

Although several nuclear plants have unexpectedly released radioactive gas or liquid to the environment and others have suffered incidents that required costly repairs, no other event in this country has approached the severity of the Three Mile Island (TMI) disaster. Some people suggest that this means the nuclear industry has fully captured the lessons learned at TMI. But closer examination of the available data reveals that even though many substantive improvements have been made in nuclear plant safety, luck is still playing a large role in protecting public health and safety.

## Initiating Events

The TMI accident began when workers making adjustments to a water purification system inadvertently stopped the cooling flow for the reactor core. The backup equipment installed specifically to cope with this situation failed. Emergency pumps designed to protect the reactor core automatically started, but the operators shut them down. They mistakenly relied on a broken instrument gauge and failed to look at a backup gauge that showed the emergency pumps were needed. The reactor core overheated, partially melted, and released more than ten million curies of radioactivity into the atmosphere.

According to the Nuclear Regulatory Commission (NRC), over the past decade US nuclear plants have reported more than 200 events very much like the one that triggered the TMI accident. The cooling water for the reactor core was unexpectedly lost in each of these events. In addition, there have been numerous other events caused by fires, pipe ruptures, and power failures. Yet none of these events led to reactor core meltdown. Why not? These events were not complicated by faulty backup equipment and worker errors as at TMI. Thus, the plants' design and operation limited these events to minor consequences. TMI was not the only potentially serious initiating event experienced by the U.S. nuclear industry. It was simply the only such event that led to an accident.

## Faulty Backup Equipment

One of the ingredients for an accident is faulty backup equipment. In recent years, the NRC and nuclear plant owners have reported several hundred instances where backup equipment was discovered to be faulty. A sampling:

- The NRC reported in July 1996 that the Haddam Neck nuclear plant in Connecticut had operated for its entire 28-year lifetime with the piping that supplies water to the reactor core too small to allow the necessary amount of water. As at TMI, the fuel in Haddam Neck's reactor core was not properly protected from severe damage by overheating.

- Two years later, the owner of the Big Rock Point nuclear plant in Michigan discovered that the facility had operated during the final third of its 39-year lifetime with the piping that would have supplied a borated solution to the reactor core completely severed. This vital emergency system would have been unable to shut down the reactor had there been an accident during this 13-year period. The borated solution is the only backup system for shutting down the reactor core. If the primary system failed, as it did at the Browns Ferry nuclear plant in 1980, the backup system would have been unable to stop the nuclear reaction.

- The owner of the Sequoyah nuclear plant reported in March 1992 that 27 of the 48 doors from the Unit 2 reactor containment building into the ice condenser would not freely open because water had gotten under the floor of the ice condenser and frozen, buckling the concrete upward several inches and blocking the doors. Further investigation revealed that 11 of the 48 ice condenser doors on Unit 1 were similarly affected. The ice condenser is a large vault containing over two million pounds of ice. The ice functions to absorb the energy released inside the reactor containment building when a pipe breaks. With so many ice condenser doors disabled, Sequoyah's reactor containment building could easily have been overpressurized and failed in event of an accident. The reactor containment building is the final barrier between radioactive material and the environment. If it failed, large amounts of radioactivity would have been released directly to the atmosphere.

- In November 1997, the NRC reported that its inspectors had found fibrous material inside the containment of the Donald C. Cook Nuclear Plant in Michigan. In case of an accident, this material may have clogged the debris screens that protect the emergency pumps. If these screens became clogged, as they did at the Perry nuclear power plant in Ohio in March 1993 and the Limerick nuclear plant in Pennsylvania during September 1995, the emergency pumps would not have been able to supply necessary cooling water to the reactor core.

- In 1997, the owner of the Quad Cities nuclear plant in Illinois informed the NRC that a fire could cut off the power to *all* of the emergency pumps and cause serious reactor core damage. Following the disastrous fire at the Browns Ferry nuclear plant in March 1975, the NRC required all owners to modify their plants to ensure that a fire could not interrupt the power to both the primary emergency pumps and their backups. More than 22 years later, the Quad Cities plant was still vulnerable. It took the plant's owners nearly a year to re-route power cables and revise emergency procedures to remedy the problems.

None of these backup equipment failures led to reactor core meltdown. Why not? These plants did not experience an initiating event, which required the backup equipment to function. Safety was achieved by not challenging the equipment rather than by having the equipment successfully fulfill the required safety functions. In other words, luck.

## Worker Errors

The remaining ingredient for an accident is worker errors. The NRC reported 728 nuclear plant problems caused by worker mistakes during a recent two-year period. That's an average of more than three mistakes per year at each nuclear plant. The Union of Concerned Scientists monitored safety performance at ten nuclear plants during 1997. The data indicated that worker errors contributed to 35 percent of the safety problems reported at the average nuclear plant. The River Bend nuclear plant in Louisiana led the list with nearly 68 percent of its safety problems involving worker mistakes. None of these worker mistakes led to reactor core meltdown. Why not? These errors were not made in conjunction with an initiating event and faulty backup equipment. It was simply a matter of timing.

## A Slot Machine Analogy

The abundance of initiating events, equipment failures, and worker mistakes can be interpreted two ways. Some argue that this data demonstrates the success of the defense-in-depth approach to safety at U.S. nuclear power plants. They maintain that backup system upon backup system and multiple barriers enable nuclear plants to tolerate problems without undue risk to the public. They suggest that the large number of reported problems shows the soundness of the defense-in-depth safety concept. They point to the fact that only one major reactor accident, Three Mile Island, has occurred in the U.S. as the ultimate proof of the industry's safety record.

This data can also be interpreted in a more ominous way. At a casino, a jackpot occurs when three spinning wheels on a slot machine all stop in a certain combination. A nuclear power plant can be compared to a slot machine having an event wheel, an equipment wheel, and a worker performance wheel. Sometimes the event wheel stops on some initiating event such as "fire," "broken pipe," or "loss of power." Sometimes the equipment wheel stops on "failure." Sometimes the worker performance wheel stops on "mistake." At Three Mile Island, the wheels stopped on "loss of feedwater," "failure," and "mistake" to produce a major reactor accident. At Chernobyl [Ukraine, where a nuclear reactor exploded], the wheels stopped on "loss of control," "failure," and "mistake" to produce another major reactor accident. Will there be another major reactor accident? The abundance of initiating events, equipment failures, and worker mistakes demonstrates that the wheels still stop frequently on these symbols. The TMI accident demonstrated that the wheels can line up for a major reactor accident.

Even the most adamant nuclear proponent must admit that a major reactor accident cannot be ruled out for the nuclear plants operating today. The key question is when will the next reactor accident occur? The NRC told the U.S. Congress in April 1985 that:

> The most complete and recent probabilistic risk assessments suggest core melt frequencies in the range of [one in one thousand] per reactor year to [one in ten thousand] per reactor year. A typical value is [three in ten thousand]. Were this the industry average, then in a population of 100 reactors operating over a period of 20 years, the crude cumulative probability of [a severe reactor] accident would be 45%.

With 103 reactors currently operating in the United States, these data suggest that a major reactor accident may be fairly likely to occur in the near future. It seems only a matter of time before the initiating event wheel, the equipment wheel, and the human performance wheel stop in a combination that produces another accident.

## Protecting the Public

Why should anyone be concerned about preventing another reactor accident? After all, the TMI accident produced some dramatic headlines and prompted a *Saturday Night Live* skit, but it did not leave portions of the Pennsylvania countryside uninhabitable. If TMI represented the worst-case reactor accident, then it might be acceptable to suffer one such disaster every generation. Unfortunately, things can be much worse than TMI. A study prepared in 1982 by the Sandia National Laboratory concluded that an accident at the Limerick nuclear plant outside Philadelphia could kill 74,000 people within the first year and cause 34,000 subsequent cancer deaths. Another 610,000 people could experience radiation-related injuries such as cataracts, temporary sterility, and thyroid nodules. The study estimated that an accident at Limerick could cost $200 billion for lost wages, relocation expenses, and decontamination efforts. The calculated results from an accident at the other nuclear plants were not as severe, but they were still significant. The study provided ample reasons for doing all that can be done to prevent another reactor accident.

What must be done to protect the public? The NRC has to rigorously enforce federal safety regulations at all nuclear plants. For example, regulations require nuclear plant owners to have programs in place to minimize the occurrence of worker mistakes and to prevent their recurrence. The high rate of personnel errors at the River Bend nuclear plant, accounting for 68 percent of the reported problems at this facility during 1997, strongly suggests that these regulations are being violated. The NRC must strictly enforce the regulations at River Bend, and at all nuclear plants, to reduce the frequency of worker mistakes. These measures will reduce the chances that the human performance wheel stops on "mistake."

In addition, the NRC must establish objective criteria to determine when a nuclear power plant with declining performance must be shut down. During the past decade, many nuclear plants, including Salem, Millstone, Clinton, D C Cook, FitzPatrick, LaSalle, Crystal River, and Indian Point 3, have been shut down for more than a year while their owners corrected numerous safety problems. Some of these safety problems required extensive repairs to emergency equipment that had been broken or improperly designed. At these plants, the equipment wheel was essentially permanently stuck on "failure." The NRC must take actions to limit the time that any plant's equipment wheel spends on "failure."

[More than] twenty years have passed since the reactor core meltdown at Three Mile Island. There have been thousands of similar initiating events, backup equipment failures, and worker mistakes in the intervening years. Fortune played a large role in preventing one or more of these initiating events from being complicated by faulty backup equipment and human errors to create another nuclear disaster. Unless actions are taken to reduce the frequency of equipment failures and worker mistakes, that era of good luck will run out. Unless these actions are taken soon, we should not bet on going another two decades without a major reactor accident.

# CHAPTER 4

# Enduring Issues and Controversies

# Nuclear Waste: The Environmental Problem That Will Not Go Away

**By Walter A. Rosenbaum**

Nuclear waste is highly toxic. Unfortunately, it is also extremely long-lived, which means it must be stored somewhere until its deadly radiation fades. As author Walter A. Rosenbaum reports in the following selection, the problem of where to permanently store nuclear waste has not been solved. It is truly a problem that will not go away. Rosenbaum is a professor of political science at the University of Florida, Gainesville. One of his most gratifying accomplishments (in his words) is introducing the first course in environmental politics in Florida and one of the first in the United States.

No problem has proven more politically troublesome to the nuclear power industry and its federal regulators than where, and how, to dispose of the enormous, highly toxic, and mounting volume of nuclear wastes in the United States. The problem, never anticipated when commercial nuclear power was first promoted, has been especially difficult because reactor wastes incite great public fear and chronic conflict among federal, state, and local officials concerning where to put them.

This nuclear waste originates from uranium mining, civilian nuclear power plants, military nuclear weapons programs, hospitals, educational institutions, and research centers. Current controversy involves four categories of waste:

- *High-Level Wastes.* This category of waste comprises highly radioactive liquids created through the reprocessing of reactor fuels. These wastes are generated by both civilian and military reactor programs. Currently, more than 100 million gallons of high-level wastes are stored in temporary containment facilities in the states of Idaho, New York, South Carolina, and Washington.

- *Transuranic Wastes.* Some of the elements in these radioactive byproducts of reactor fuel and military waste processing remain dangerous for extraordinarily long periods. Plutonium-239, with a half-life of 24,000 years, and americum-243, with a 7,300-year half-life, are among the transuranics. Other more exotic transuranic elements have a half-life exceeding 200,000 years.
- *Spent Nuclear Fuel.* About 32,000 metric tons of spent fuel, mostly from civilian reactors, are stored temporarily in cooling ponds at reactor sites. By 2000 this spent fuel increased to more than 42,000 metric tons.
- *Low-Level Wastes.* Any material contaminated by radiation and emitting low levels of radioactivity itself belongs in this category. This includes workers' clothing, tools, equipment, and other items associated with nuclear reactors or nuclear materials. Low-level wastes currently are stored at repositories in Nevada, New York, and South Carolina. . . .

## Storing Waste

In the early years of nuclear power promotion, it was assumed that spent fuel from civilian and military plants would be reprocessed: the fissionable materials, primarily plutonium, would be recovered for use again as reactor fuel, and the remaining high-level waste eventually would be contained and isolated at appropriate disposal sites. In the planners' early view, the high-level and transuranic wastes remaining after reprocessing posed a largely technical and readily solvable problem of finding the appropriate containment materials and geographic location for permanent storage. They did not anticipate the failure of civilian reprocessing and the resulting volume of nuclear waste. They did not foresee the necessity to store military wastes for decades longer than the containment structures were designed to last. They did not anticipate the political repercussions in trying to find a place to put the waste.

Existing and planned commercial facilities were designed to

store temporarily no more than three years' worth of accumulated spent fuel in cooling ponds until the fuel assemblies were reprocessed. Since the early 1970s, however, virtually all spent fuel has been stored in these cooling ponds. Space and time are now running out. The United States continues to reprocess its spent military fuel, thereby generating most of the high-level liquid wastes accumulating at military nuclear reservations. Until 1982 the federal government had no comprehensive plan for the permanent storage of these nuclear wastes. The federal government and the states quarreled for more than a decade over how a permanent waste depository would be designed and which states would be depository sites—nobody wanted it. Idaho and South Carolina, already accommodating large volumes of high- and low-level wastes from other states, were increasingly reluctant to accept more. In 1976 California ordered a moratorium on the construction of commercial nuclear facilities until Washington, D.C., could certify that a permanent repository for their spent fuel existed. The nuclear waste issue was approaching a crisis.

## The States Play Nuclear "Keep Away"

In 1982 Congress finally passed the Nuclear Waste Policy Act (NWPA), which was intended to create a process for designating and constructing the first permanent repositories for nuclear waste. The act appeared to end a decade of nasty legislative infighting during which each state scrambled to write language into the law ensuring that it would not be a candidate for the repository. The legislation assigned the site-selection task to the Department of Energy (DOE) and created what appeared to be a meticulously detailed, impartial, and open process by which all possible sites would be thoroughly studied and reduced to a few from which the president would eventually select two, one east and one west of the Mississippi River. The president was to designate the first site by March 31, 1987, and the second by July 1, 1989. To demonstrate its confidence in the process, the DOE agreed to begin accepting high-level commercial wastes sometime in 1998.

Following procedures required by the NWPA, the DOE in 1985 nominated three permanent western sites to the president from which he was to select one: Deaf Smith County, Texas; the Hartford Nuclear Reservation in Washington state; and Yucca Mountain, Nevada (near the Nevada atomic test site). Every stage of the designation process, however, was accompanied by political fire-works. Republican senators and representatives from each desig-nated state complained to the White House that the designation of their state would penalize the party at the polls in 1986 and 1988. The political leadership of both parties in all three states com-plained bitterly that their states had been improperly designated and attempted to overturn the designation in the courts. Environ-mental groups in each state went to court, challenging the desig-nations on technical and procedural grounds. And Congress antic-ipated another rancorous round when the president was scheduled to select the second repository site from a set of states in 1989.

Rather than abide the continuing controversy, Congress found a simpler solution to the designation problem. In December 1987 Congress suddenly renounced the procedures it had ordered in the NWPA and summarily designated Nevada to be the first permanent waste site. As a consolation, Nevada was assured up to $20 million annually to manage the job. Nevada legislators were outraged. It "will turn our state into a federal colony," accused Republican rep-resentative Barbara F. Vucanovich. "Instead of leadership and prin-ciple, it's a gang-rape mentality," added a spokesperson for Richard Bryan, Nevada's governor. The man who arranged it all thought oth-erwise. "If I were a Nevadan living in the real world, I would be happy with this bill," asserted Sen. J. Bennett Johnston, D-La. "I would bet that in a very few years, Nevada will deem this one of their most treasured industries." Throughout the 1990s, however, Nevada continued to resist development of the Yucca Mountain fa-cility with every political resource it had available.

This trench warfare slowed the facility's construction to a crawl, but Congress in 1997 left little doubt that Nevada was still the na-tion's most eligible nuclear waste bin. Both the House and the Senate passed legislation, over the state's vehement objections, that would create a temporary repository near the Yucca Mountain site for the high-level nuclear waste still awaiting the completion of the permanent Nevada site. In the keep-away politics of nuclear waste, the most weakly defended constituency was still "it."

## Repository Problems

"It's fair to say we've solved the nuclear waste problem with this legislation," Senator Johnston assured his colleagues with prema-ture optimism after they awarded the waste to Nevada. But after more than two years of preliminary work and an expenditure of $500 million at the Nevada site, the DOE announced in 1989 that it was abandoning its initial repository plan because it lacked confidence in the technical quality of the proposal. The DOE predicted that the repository would be delayed until at least 2010, even though it was committed to accepting high-level wastes from commercial reactors by 1998 and the commercial utilities had already paid $3 billion in taxes to use the repository. However, by 1998 it was evident that the DOE would not be ready to receive the wastes at even a temporary repository, and the availability of a permanent repository remained equally speculative. "A realistic date for having a permanent repository operational keeps receding farther into the future," concluded the GAO [General Accounting Office].

Meanwhile, reports on the DOE's nuclear waste management projects have been unrelieved bad news since the late 1980s. In mid-1989 the DOE announced that it was delaying the opening of its Waste Isolation Pilot Project (WIPP) near Carlsbad, New Mexico. The WIPP, begun in the late 1970s, was intended to store the plutonium wastes generated at the Rocky Flats nuclear military facility near Denver, Colorado, where space for the liquid wastes was fast disappearing. The underground repository had been scheduled to receive its first shipments in 1992, but the DOE's scientific advisers urged a delay of two or three years because the DOE needed to complete technical diagrams of twenty-one systems already built into the structure, including the electrical, radiation control, and fire protection systems. In fact, the WIPP did not receive its first nuclear waste until 2001.

The WIPP's delay added another chapter to the already protracted, acrimonious debate about the safety of that facility and raised doubts that the WIPP will ever be used. Thus, the nation still lacks a permanent repository for its civilian and military nuclear wastes. Waste storage capacity at civilian utility sites continues to dwindle. At the same time, military waste-containment structures are deteriorating dangerously at places such as the Hanford Nuclear Reservation, where 440,000 cubic yards of high-, low-, and extremely long-lived nuclear wastes are stored, some since 1943, awaiting permanent disposition. This is not, however, the whole of the national nuclear waste problem. The controversy attending reactor waste deflects public attention from the emerging problem of disposing of nuclear facilities themselves after they have outlived their usefulness.

# Decommissioning Problems

Once a civilian or military nuclear facility has finished its useful life, the NRC and the DOE require that the owners decommission the facility by removing from the site the radioactive materials, including land, groundwater, buildings, contents, and equipment, and by reducing residual radioactivity to a level permitting the property to be used for any other purpose. Because a commercial reactor's life span is expected to be fifty years, an increasing number of the nation's reactors had to be decommissioned beginning in the 1990s. However, no utility has yet decommissioned a large plant, and none expect to do so until a permanent high-level waste depository is available. Instead, the utilities plan to partially decommission their facilities and to put them in so-called safe storage while awaiting the completion of a permanent repository.

In fact, little is known about how large facilities can be taken apart and rendered safe. Few of the nation's utilities have done much practical planning for decommissioning their own plants. No reliable estimates are available for decommissioning costs, which have been calculated to range from tens of millions to $3 billion for each facility. The NRC currently requires utilities to set aside $105 million to $135 million for decommissioning, but many experts believe these estimates are too low. Utilities are also required to have decommissioning plans, cost estimates, or written certification that they will meet NRC's cost estimates. Still, no utility has yet created a decommissioning fund, assessed its rate payers for the costs, or filed a decommissioning plan with the NRC in the absence of a permanent high-level waste repository.

The DOE's responsibility for decommissioning the nation's military reactors presents even more formidable problems. Investigations of the nation's military nuclear facility management in the late 1980s revealed appalling negligence in waste storage and management, leaks of dangerous radioactive materials for decades into the surrounding environment and civilian settlements, and deceit and secrecy in managing information about the lethal dangers created both on- and offsite from waste mismanagement. This legacy of negligence leaves the DOE with a conservatively estimated cost of $230 billion to decontaminate and decommission its nuclear facilities. Many experts believe the costs will climb much higher, so intolerably high that the sites will be, as some plant engineers privately predict, "national sacrifice zones" never adequately decontaminated.

Waste management and nuclear plant decommissioning problems will trouble Americans for centuries and remain a reminder of the technological optimism and mission fixation that inspired Washington, D.C.'s approach to nuclear technology development. Indeed, the politics of civilian nuclear power development has been as important as its science in shaping the economic, ecological, and technological character of the industry. So it will continue to be. The future of commercial nuclear power will be determined, in good part, by how Congress, the White House, and the NRC respond to its present ills and challenges. The battle for the nuclear future is still being fought in these political arenas.

# Atomic Energy Is Environmentally Friendly

**By Bertram David Wolfe**

In the following article Bertram David Wolfe argues that nuclear energy is the most viable and realistic option for keeping up with global energy demand. For the United States, an emphasis on atomic energy will also improve international relations (by reducing America's dependence on foreign oil) and reduce greenhouse gases and other pollutants. Although the buildup of nuclear waste is a shortcoming of more nuclear power, Wolfe believes the problem can be solved. Wolfe is a consultant and former vice president and general manager of General Electric's nuclear energy division as well as former president of the American Nuclear Society.

It may be the only viable energy option that can prevent economic stagnation, energy conflicts, and environmental degradation.

## The Global Demand for Energy

Third World population growth and economic development are setting the stage for an energy crisis in the next century. By midcentury the Third World population will double from 4 billion to 8 billion people, while the population of the industrial world will grow by about 20 percent to 1.2 billion. Impoverished Third World people today use less than one-tenth as much energy per capita as do U.S. citizens. Unless we expect to see the majority of the world's people living indefinitely in dire poverty, we should be

Bertram David Wolfe, "Why Environmentalists Should Promote Nuclear Energy," *Issues in Science and Technology*, vol. 12, Summer 1996. Copyright © 1996 by the University of Texas at Dallas, Richardson, TX. Reproduced by permission.

prepared for per capita energy use to rise rapidly with economic progress. Even if Third World per capita energy use rises to only one-third of the U.S. level, that increase in combination with expected population growth will result in a threefold increase in world energy use by 2050.

If fossil fuels are used to supply this increased energy need, we can expect serious deterioration of air quality and possible environmental disaster from global climate change due to the greenhouse effect. In addition, increased demand for fossil fuels combined with dwindling supplies will lead to higher prices, slowed economic growth, and the likelihood of energy-related global conflicts. Does anyone doubt that Kuwait's oil resources were a major factor in U.S. willingness to take military action against Iraq? Increased competition for fossil fuels will only exacerbate tensions.

Alternatives to this scenario are few. Perhaps future world energy use can be stabilized at a level much less than a third of present U.S. per capita use. (Of course, the demand could be much higher.) Perhaps solar or wind power will become practical on a large scale. Perhaps fusion, or even cold fusion, will be developed. Perhaps some new, clean, plentiful energy source will emerge. We can all hope for an easy answer to our energy needs, but it is irresponsible to base our future on such hopes.

But if we limit our planning to proven and reliable energy technologies with adequate fuel supplies and low environmental risks that we know can meet the world's energy needs in the 21st century, we must focus on nuclear power. However, even conventional nuclear power plants will face fuel supply problems in the next century if their use expands significantly. Fortunately, we also have experience with nuclear breeder reactors, such as the Advanced Liquid Metal Reactor (ALMR), that can produce more than a hundred times as much energy per pound of uranium as do conventional reactors.

The United States has been a leader in the development of nuclear power technology and the adoption of stringent safety standards. Not a single member of the public has been harmed by the operation of any of the world's nuclear plants that meet U.S. standards. (The Chernobyl reactor [which exploded in Ukraine in 1986], which lacked a containment structure, did not meet U.S. standards.) The United States has also been successful in using its peaceful nuclear power leadership to limit the worldwide spread of nuclear weapons.

But the future of nuclear energy in the United States is now in question. Since 1973, all new nuclear energy plant orders have subsequently been canceled. In 1993, U.S. utilities shut down three nuclear energy plants rather than invest in needed repairs. Of the 110 presently operating U.S. nuclear energy plants, 45 will reach the end of their planned 40-year life-time in the next two decades, and there are no plans for replacing them with new nuclear energy plants. Indeed, the utility industry seems to have no interest in even thinking about building new nuclear power plants. Not a single U.S. utility responded to a Nuclear Regulatory Commission (NRC) request to test a proposed new procedure for early approval of a new nuclear energy plant site even though no commitment for actual site use was required. And the [Bill] Clinton administration . . . canceled support for advanced nuclear energy development programs, including the ALMR program.

This is the wrong time for the nation or the world to ignore nuclear power. Demand for energy will grow, and our options are limited. Ironically, environmentalists, who have opposed nuclear power since the 1970s, should have the strongest rationale for promoting nuclear energy. Like almost all large endeavors, nuclear power has its problems and its risks. But the problems of nuclear power do not look so bad when compared with the air pollution, global warming, and the supply limitations associated with fossil fuels. Besides, the major drawbacks of nuclear power—from cost to waste disposal—are due more to institutional impediments than to technological difficulties. Considering the growth in energy demand and the risks associated with other energy sources, the benefit-risk ratio for nuclear power is very attractive. Indeed, the welfare of our future generations and the environment may depend on maintaining the viability of nuclear power.

## An Energy Surplus

Peaceful nuclear power began in 1954 with President [Dwight] Eisenhower's "Atoms For Peace" program. A major goal was to inhibit the spread of nuclear weapons by trading peaceful nuclear power knowledge and technology for agreements to refrain from nuclear weapons development. During this period it was estimated that some 20 nations had initiated nuclear programs, and President Eisenhower's concern was that the "knowledge possessed by several nations will eventually be shared by others—possibly all others." In view of the lack of weapons use and the small number of nations with nuclear weapons today, one can characterize the Atoms for Peace program as a major success. Of course, our experience with Iraq, North Korea, and South Africa makes it clear that diligence must be maintained.

Peaceful nuclear power development started slowly in the late 1950s with initial demonstration plants, but by the mid- to late-1960s commercial nuclear power plant orders began to take off, and by the early 1970s some 30 to 40 nuclear energy plants were being ordered each year. It was projected that the United States would have more than a thousand nuclear energy plants in operation by the end of the century.

This bullish outlook resulted from several factors. The first was that electricity use was growing at the rate of about 7 percent per year, leading to a need for a doubling of electrical capacity every 10 years. At the same time, there was a growing awareness among utility executives of the pollution effects of fossil-fuel burning. Responding to the very negative public reactions to his company's announcement that it would be starting up a new coal-fired plant in 1961, McChesney Martin, chairman of Florida Power and Light (FP&L), promised never to build another coal plant. Shortly thereafter, FP&L committed to build the Turkey Point Nuclear Station. In the mid-1960s, the Sierra Club became a major supporter of the Diablo Canyon Nuclear Plant in California.

This period of rapid nuclear expansion and environmentalist support of nuclear power ended in 1973 after the Arab oil boycott. As a result of the boycott, the cost of oil went from $2 to $12 a barrel. This drove up the price of electricity, which led to economic disruption and a dramatic slowdown in the growth of demand for electricity. The rate of growth fell to 2 percent a year, a doubling of use every 35 years. Because of the prior ordering to meet the anticipated 10-year doubling time, there has been until very recently a surplus of electric-generation capacity. This surplus was maintained despite the post-1973 cancellations of 108 nuclear and 93 fossil-fuel plants that were on order.

This surplus has distorted the nation's perspective on energy in general and nuclear energy in particular. During this period of surplus, one could find fault with virtually all energy sources; coal, oil, natural gas, hydroelectricity, and nuclear power could all be judged unacceptable because there was no need for new plants. A number of environmental organizations such as Greenpeace and the Sierra Club insisted that the nation should hold out for ideal or risk-free sources such as energy conservation, solar power, and wind energy. It didn't matter if interminable delays were imposed on the construction of new power plants because there was no pressing need for the electricity. No one suffered from a shortage of electricity as the construction time for a nuclear power plant expanded from 4-to-6 years to 10-to-15 years or even longer.

These extended construction times have been ascribed to an ever more complicated and inefficient regulatory licensing system and to court delays resulting from suits brought by those opposed to nuclear power. Although these did indeed contribute to the delays, in my view the underlying cause was lack of need. In Japan and France, for example, where demand for electricity continued to grow rapidly, new nuclear energy plants of U.S. design are still being licensed and built in four to six years. I question whether NRC or the courts (or for that matter Congress) would have tolerated the delays if new electricity was truly needed. One real result of the delays, however, was that the cost of building a nuclear plant in the United States increased dramatically, making nuclear power uncompetitive and unattractive to investors.

## Environmental Benefits

Although the rate of growth of electricity use declined after 1973, demand did increase as the economy expanded. U.S. electricity use increased 70 percent between 1973 and 1994, while the gross domestic product grew by 63 percent. The new demand was met primarily by new plants, predominantly coal and nuclear, that were ordered before 1973 and constructed in the two decades following. Coal generation doubled between 1973 and 1994, and today provides over 50 percent of U.S. electricity. The 74 nuclear energy plants that came on line in this period increased nuclear's share of electricity generation from 4 percent in 1973 to more than 20 percent today, second only to coal. The other sources are natural gas (14 percent); hydropower (9 percent); wood, wind, and solar (3 percent); and oil (3 percent). The added nuclear capacity allowed for the shutdown of oil-fired plants, permitting the utilities to reduce oil imports by some 100 million barrels per year and thus lower the trade deficit by over a billion dollars per year. The substitution of nuclear for fossil-fueled plants has reduced present $CO_2$ [carbon dioxide] atmospheric emissions by more than 130 million metric tons of carbon per year, roughly 10 percent of to-tal U.S. $CO^2$ production. Nevertheless, the United States still needs to reduce carbon production by an additional 10 percent to reach its goal of returning to the 1990 production level. In addition, re-placement of fossil-fuel plants with nuclear power has reduced ni-trogen oxide emissions to the air by over 2 million tons annually, meeting the goal set by the Clean Air Act for the year 2000, and has reduced sulfur dioxide emissions by almost 5 million tons per year, half the goal for the year 2000. Both nitrogen oxide and sul-fur dioxide are harmful to human health and the environment.

U.S. nuclear power plants themselves have an admirable envi-ronmental and public health record. Safety has been a critical con-sideration in plant design from the beginning. Standard operation of a nuclear plant produces no ill effects, and even in the case of a major malfunction or accident, the use of a containment structure that surrounds the plant prevents the release of significant amounts of radioactive material. The wisdom of the U.S. approach is evi-dent in a comparison of the accidents at the Three Mile Island plant in Pennsylvania [in 1979] and the Soviet Union's Chernobyl reac-tor. Thanks to the containment structure, not a single member of the public was injured by nuclear radiation from the Three Mile Is-land accident. In fact, a person standing outside the plant would have received less radiation exposure from it than from a two-week vacation in high-altitude Denver with its uranium-rich soil. Signif-icant harm to humans resulted from the accident at the Chernobyl plant, which lacked a containment structure.

## Solving the Waste Problem

One commonly cited drawback of nuclear power is that it creates radioactive waste that must be contained for thousands of years. Nuclear waste is a serious concern, but one that can be success-fully managed and is less worrisome than the emissions from fossil-fuel plants. Coal, gas, wood, and oil plants emit greenhouse gases and other undesirable materials to the environment. No nu-clear wastes are directly emitted to the environment. Of course, radioactive waste can represent a serious hazard if it is not prop-erly maintained, but its small volume allows very high expendi-tures and great care per unit volume. If all the country's high-level nuclear waste from over three decades of plant operations were collected on a football field, it would be only 9 feet deep. Nuclear power plant wastes have been carefully maintained at the plants for decades without harm to the environment or the public. Because high-level waste, composed largely of spent nuclear fuel, remains radioactive for thousands of years, the plan is to seal this waste in sturdy containers and bury it in underground geological structures that have remained stable for millions of years. The feasibility of this approach has been supported by a large number of national and international studies.

After the Department of Energy considered a number of possible storage sites for the waste and made its recommendations, Congress selected Yucca Mountain, Nevada, which is adjacent to a nuclear weapons testing site, as the place for the first high-level waste repository. Extensive underground exploration of the site and evaluation of its geology is now under way. If this research finds that the site is suitable, the repository will begin operation in the period from 2010 to 2020. In the meantime, the used fuel can be safely stored indefinitely in above-ground facilities.

Progress toward permanent storage of low-level waste from nuclear energy plants, medical procedures, and industrial processes, which is less radioactive and loses its radioactivity within a few hundred years, has also been slow. In 1987, Congress passed a law giving responsibility for management of the low-level wastes to the states. What has happened since then in California is an example of the institutional barriers impeding nuclear power development.

After extensive study, California chose a site in Ward Valley in the Mojave desert. The California Department of Health Services spent several years reviewing the site and the design of the repository, with ample opportunities for public input. In 1993, it approved the site and design. Unfortunately, the site is on federal land, which must be transferred to the state before it can be used for the repository. Secretary of the Interior Bruce Babbitt insisted on an independent review by the National Research Council before making the transfer. This year-long study concluded in May 1995 that the site was suitable for the repository. Similar conclusions were also reached by the Bureau of Land Management and the U.S. Geological Survey. Nevertheless, because of pressure from antinuclear organizations, the site has still not been transferred, and it is not clear how long the delay will be. In the meantime, the low-level wastes, including medical and industrial wastes, are being held at many temporary storage sites in the state. These sites could raise safety problems that would easily be avoided by opening the Ward Valley Repository.

There is no guarantee of absolute safety with nuclear wastes or with any potentially hazardous substance. Numerous expert studies have found that Yucca Mountain and Ward Valley provide the safety needed by the public. But as long as our institutional processes make it easy to stop the development of repositories on the basis of insubstantial doubts about safety, we will not be able to move from temporary storage to a safer, permanent solution. We are moving in the right direction, but the pace is unnecessarily slow. And while antinuclear activists continue to quibble about the possibility of some future hazard, we continue to pollute the air with fossil fuel emissions that cause tens of thousands of premature deaths each year in the United States and produce greenhouse gases that could lead to global climate change with potentially disastrous consequences. Are some environmental Neros fiddling while Rome burns?

And if high-level radioactive waste is such a serious problem, doesn't it make sense to revive developmental support for the ALMR reactor, which "burns" or transmutes the long-lived radioactive materials, so that after a few hundred years the wastes become less hazardous than the natural uranium in the ground?

## Reviving Nuclear Power

As the damaging effects of fossil fuels become more apparent and the need for additional electric generating capacity increases, the time for dismissing nuclear power is coming to an end. The current generation of U.S. nuclear power plants has performed well, and an even better generation of new designs is ready. General Electric, in partnership with Hitachi and Toshiba, has developed the Advanced Boiling Water Reactor (ABWR), which incorporates lessons learned from earlier designs. Construction of the first ABWR began in Japan in 1991, and the plant is already operating at full power. The ability to build and begin operation of a new design in less than five years is a testament to the quality of construction and the regulatory system in Japan. Combustion Engineering, which has been building its System 80 nuclear plants in South Korea in less than six years, is ready to move forward with its improved System 80+. Both of these new designs have already gone through more than six years of evaluation by NRC, receiving favorable reviews and approvals.

In addition to these evolutionary new designs, several companies have been working on passively safe designs, which it is hoped will provide even greater protection in the event of an accident. Westinghouse's AP600 and the technology of General Electric's Simplified Boiling Water Reactor (SBWR) are moving forward, but neither design is ready for commercial construction. Although there are people who argue that we should wait for such designs to be ready before building any new nuclear plants in the United States, currently available designs do not pose a safety problem and are safer than the alternative of increased fossil fuel use. Thus, there is no practical reason to wait for a new design that is theoretically safer but has its own development problems.

Reviews of the new commercially available designs indicate that they will have favorable safety, operating, and economic characteristics compared to fossil plants if (and this is a big if) they can be built as efficiently here as they are in other countries. But experience with the U.S. licensing and court review procedures suggests that it can take two to four times as long to construct a nuclear plant in the United States as it does abroad, with exorbitant increases in cost.

One reason for the long construction times is that in the past each U.S. plant had to go through the full review process, even if it was a replica of a previously built plant. In addition, much of the review took place during construction. Aware of this problem, the NRC, the nuclear industry, and Congress have developed a new "standardized" licensing procedure intended to eliminate the delays. Under this procedure, the NRC reviews the design and construction procedures in detail and evaluates critical comments from those opposed to the plant design or construction before construction is allowed to start. If a standardized license is granted, multiple plants of the same design can be built with the only licensing requirement being to demonstrate that the construction was performed in accordance with the license.

The problem is that this new licensing system has not yet been demonstrated to work as intended. Can it withstand the efforts of opponents of nuclear power who will use the legal system in any way that they can to stop or slow construction of a new nuclear power plant? Who can predict the timing of court rulings and appeals? Despite the fact that the new licensing procedure is intended to let construction continue during the court proceedings, what company would risk proceeding with a multibillion-dollar project with so little certainty about if and when it will be completed?

The private sector will not proceed with a new nuclear project without evidence that the new licensing system works. This is likely to require that a demonstration project or two be initiated whose licensing risks are underwritten by the government and/or shared by a number of power utilities. The U.S. government, for example, might agree to underwrite the added costs of the first demonstration plants if they encounter delays that the new licensing system is intended to eliminate. Similarly, utilities who feel a responsibility to provide for their customers' future might enter into a joint demonstration project and share the risks and (hopefully) the benefits.

Japan, Korea, and France have demonstrated that nuclear power plants that meet U.S. standards can be built economically in four to six years. Thus our problem is clearly not technical but institutional: Can we build U.S.-designed plants as efficiently in the United States as we do abroad? Our government should eliminate bureaucratic impediments that serve only as tools for those philosophically opposed to nuclear power.

## Long-Term Needs

The world must be prepared for the increasing energy needs in the next century and beyond. The U.S.-led ALMR program was intended to develop a safe, economical, proliferation-resistant, essentially unlimited energy supply for the future. The program was proceeding well, with reactor design and fuel cycle development making substantial progress. As we have learned from past experience with light water reactors, it takes decades to uncover and solve the long-term problems of a new nuclear system. Thus, to be ready for the energy needs projected in the next century, the ALMR development program should be vigorously pursued now. Private companies cannot take on such an expensive and slow-maturing project. Government must fund the project at this stage.

Unfortunately, the program has been canceled because of concern that the use of plutonium could lead to the proliferation of nuclear weapons. Although it is true that the use of breeder reactors in the United States would result in the creation of more plutonium, a U.S. decision to forego breeder reactors will not affect other countries that see the need for breeders in the future and continue to develop and operate them. The major effect of our abandonment of the ALMR program will be loss of U.S. leadership and influence in its future development as well as the loss of our leadership in assuring a proliferation-resistant fuel cycle. Besides, the failure to provide adequate and affordable electricity for future economic needs is a much more serious threat to world peace. Indeed, competition and potential hostilities over scarce energy supplies increase the threat that nuclear weapons will be acquired—and used.

None of these policy changes will be made without a change in the public's attitude toward nuclear power. People need to understand the need for additional future energy supplies; the problems of fossil fuels; and the relative safety, reliability, and environmental advantages of nuclear power. The nuclear industry has done a poor job of educating the public about nuclear energy. And because of its perceived economic stake, the nuclear industry may not be a credible carrier for this message. More disinterested voices, particularly those in the environmental community, should be heard. The Club of Rome, an international organization with a particular interest in preserving the environment, has evolved from nuclear critic to nuclear promoter because of its concern about global climate change. U.S. environmentalists need to take a fresh look at world and national energy needs, the clear and worsening problems of fossil fuels, and the empirical evidence about the safety of nuclear power.

# Atomic Energy Is Expensive

## By Amory B. and L. Hunter Lovins

According to Amory B. and L. Hunter Lovins, nuclear power is dead: It cannot compete in the marketplace against other inexpensive energy sources such as superefficient gas plants or wind power. They also believe energy-efficient appliances and other new technologies will decrease energy demand, thus lessening the need for nuclear power. Amory B. and L. Hunter Lovins are founders and co-CEOs of the Rocky Mountain Institute, a nonprofit, natural resource think tank. The *Wall Street Journal* named Amory B. Lovins one of the twenty-eight people worldwide most likely to change the course of business in the 1990s.

**B**uoyed by a supportive White House, growing climate concerns, temporarily high gas prices, and California's electricity mess, the nuclear industry is running an all-out public-relations campaign to resuscitate its product. This attempt ignores one crucial fact: Nuclear power already died of an incurable attack of market forces. Once touted as "too cheap to meter," nuclear power, as *The Economist* recently concluded, now looks "too costly to matter."

## Uncompetitive and Unnecessary

Overwhelmed by huge construction and repair costs around the world, nuclear plants ended up achieving less than 10% of the capacity and 1% of the new orders (all from countries with centrally planned energy systems) forecast a quarter-century ago. The industry has suffered the greatest collapse of any enterprise in industrial history. Beyond the hard economic facts, about which more later, the nuclear industry is dismissing legitimate public concerns about the risks of a technology so unforgiving that, as Nobel physicist Hannes Alfven wrote, "No acts of God can be permitted." Each nuclear plant, through accident or malice, could release enough radioactivity to hazard a continent. This is presented by the industry as extremely unlikely, but many citizens aren't reassured. They have seen too many highly improbable events, including terrorism. And if nuclear power plants are so safe, why would the industry build and run them only if the federal government passed a law limiting operators' liability in major accidents? Why should the nuclear industry enjoy a liability cap that reduces its incentive for safety, distorts choices with a vast subsidy and is unavailable to any other industry? Why can't nuclear operators self-insure and put their money where their mouths are, or buy insurance at market prices like everyone else? The liability law's expiration in 2002 presents an awkward dilemma for advocates of both nuclear power and free markets.

Scientists still haven't developed reliable ways to handle nuclear wastes and decommissioned plants, which remain dangerously radioactive for far longer than societies last or geological foresight extends. And experts feel nuclear power's gravest risk is that power plants can provide ingredients and innocent-seeming civilian cover for the development of nuclear bombs, as was the case in India and elsewhere. Now the White House proposes to revive nuclear-fuel reprocessing after decades of proof that it's unprofitable, unnecessary, a complication to nuclear waste management and a source of vast amounts of bomb material.

Market economics provides an even more basic argument: "If a thing is not worth doing," said economist John Maynard Keynes, "it is not worth doing well." Leaving aside bomb-proliferation, waste, sabotage and uninsurable accidents, nuclear power is simply uncompetitive and unnecessary. After a trillion-dollar taxpayer investment, it delivers little more energy in the U.S. than wood. Globally, it produces severalfold less energy than renewable sources. The market prefers other options. In the 1990s, global nuclear capacity rose by 1% a year, compared with 17% for solar cells (24% last year) and 24% for wind power—which has lately added about 5,000 megawatts a year worldwide, as compared with the 3,100 new megawatts nuclear power averaged annually in the 1990s. The decentralized generators California added in the 1990s have more capacity than its two giant nuclear plants—whose debts triggered the restructuring that created the state's current utility mess.

## Non-Nuclear Options

Enthusiasts claim new-style reactors might deliver a kilowatt-hour to your meter for 5 cents, compared with 10 to 15 cents for post-1980 nuclear plants worldwide. (Of that, 10 to 15 cents, nearly 3 cents pays for delivery, about 2 cents for running the plant, and the rest for its construction and for occasional major repairs.) But on the same accounting basis, superefficient gas plants or wind farms cost only 5 to 6 cents per kilowatt-hour, co-generation of heat and power often 1 to 5 cents, and efficient lights, motors and other electricity-saving devices under 2 cents, often under 1 cent. Cogeneration and efficiency are especially cheap because they occur at the site where the energy is consumed and thus require no delivery.

All these non-nuclear options continue to get cheaper, as do fuel cells and solar cells. Today, a pound of silicon can produce more electricity than a pound of nuclear fuel. Already, Sacramento's municipal utility, which has successfully replaced power from its ailing nuclear plant (shut down by voters) with a portfolio emphasizing efficiency and renewables, has brought the heretofore costliest option, solar cells, down to costs competitive with a new nuclear plant.

The PR [public relations] spinners trumpet that nuclear power costs less than power from gas plants. This is true if you are looking only at the running cost of an average existing nuclear plant, compared with the running costs of an old, inefficient gas-fired plant. It does not include delivery to customers, nor the prohibitive construction costs of a new nuclear plant. Notice, too, the ads don't compare the costs of a new nuclear plant with the new, doubled-efficiency gas plants that are beating the pants off nuclear and coal worldwide. Under such realistic cost comparisons, nuclear power plummets to its actual status as the worst buy available. You didn't understand that from those slick ads? You weren't supposed to. The nuclear industry has a well-earned reputation for breezy mendacity.

## Reducing Demand, Increasing Efficiency

Lost in the debate over what kind of new plant to build is the best option of all: more efficient use of the electricity we already have. We've been reducing electricity use per dollar of gross domestic product by 1.6% a year nationwide, and in California between 1997 and 2000, by 4.4% a year. California has held its per-capita electricity use essentially flat since the mid-1970s, yet far more savings remain untapped—enough nationally to save four times nuclear power's output, at one-sixth its operating cost. Our personal household electric bill, for example, is $5 a month for a 4,000-square-foot house in the Rocky Mountains. Passive solar design and super-efficient appliances and lighting yielded a 90% savings on electricity and 99% on fuel. The improvements, made in 1983, paid for themselves in 10 months. Today's technologies are far better. An estimated three-fourths of U.S. electricity could now be saved through efficiency techniques that cost less than generating that power, even in existing plants.

Nor, finally, do shortages of electricity in California justify more nuclear plants anywhere. California did not have soaring electricity demand during the 1990s, did not stop building power plants and is probably not even short of generating capacity. The system that had rolling blackouts at a 28-gigawatt load [in] winter [2001] is the same one that comfortably delivered 53 gigawatts two summers ago. Half its power plants didn't suddenly evaporate. Rather, there's apparently been adequate generating capacity—if power plants ran as reliably as they did before utilities sold them. But in fact, since utility maintenance contracts expired [in] fall [2000] many of the sold plants have been calling in sick—often, some evidence suggests, because their new owners earn far more profit by selling less electricity at a higher price rather than more at a lower price.

If California does have a serious supply-demand imbalance, it should be resolved in the cheapest, fastest, surest and safest ways. Buying more nuclear plants violates all these criteria. It would buy less solution per dollar, making the problem worse. That's also true of nuclear solutions to climate change.

Anyone who doubts the effectiveness of demand-side solutions need only to look to California, where in the first half of [2001] with limited formal programs, Californians have decreased their peak demand for electricity by more than 12%, reversing the past 5 to 10 years' growth in demand.

After a half-century of nuclear power, the verdict of the marketplace is in. Nuclear power has flunked the market test. Nuclear salesmen scour the world for a single order, while makers of alternatives enjoy brisk business. Let's profit from their experience. Taking markets seriously, not propping up failed technologies at public expense, offers a stable climate, a prosperous economy, and a cleaner and more peaceful world.

# Atomic Energy Is Cheap

**By Robert C. Morris**

According to Robert C. Morris, antinuclear activists have kept the United States from achieving its economic potential in the marketplace. Nuclear power, he argues, is the cheapest source of energy, but those who oppose it have driven up its costs by lobbying for unnecessary and expensive regulations on nuclear plant operation. Morris is a retired chemistry teacher, educational consultant, and former chairman of the science department for Illinois High School District 88.

**H**ave you or someone in your family lost their job or been forced to take a cut in pay? If so, maybe the antinuclear activists are to blame.

Almost every imaginable product requires some energy for its production. In the case of a red-hot steel ingot being rolled into sheet steel, it's easy to see the energy component.

But, it's not so easy to visualize the energy which went into the production of say, a hamburger. While the cattle were out on the range, coal generated electricity may have been used to pump the livestock's water tanks full of water. Then, diesel powered trucks transported the animals to the packing plant. Once there, electrical energy lit the plant, moved the conveyer belts, and kept the entire plant and the refrigerators cold enough so that the meat wouldn't spoil. A refrigerated truck moved the freshly ground beef to a wholesaler, and, later, on to the restaurant's walk-in coolers. Finally, a gas or electric grill was used to cook the burger. Of course, electric signs were needed to attract customers, and electric lights were used to keep the store brightly lit. And, the building had to be heated or cooled, so more natural gas or electrical energy was needed. All of this energy costs money, and a small bit of it is recaptured with each hamburger sold.

In some industries, the cost of energy may be as much as 50 percent of the total cost of the product. Obviously, the cost of energy can determine whether a product succeeds—or fails—in the marketplace.

Until recently, Americans enjoyed the advantage of having access to some of the world's cheapest energy. We had ample supplies of coal and oil within our borders, so shipping costs were low. Once the U.S. monopolies were broken up, U.S. oil and coal companies competed with each other for sales, and this competition kept the price low. In turn, these low energy costs fueled our growth and prosperity. The energy component of our goods was small, and they sold well on the world market. For a long time, we enjoyed the advantage of oil which cost less than $1.80 a barrel. Then came OPEC, and today oil is $19.00 a barrel.

However, OPEC isn't the only threat to our prosperity. The antinuclear activists pose an even bigger threat to our economy, and not every country is equally threatened by them. In those countries where it has been possible to control these militant groups, the use of nuclear power has grown more rapidly than it has in the U.S., which explains why 18 countries now use nuclear power to generate a higher percentage of their electricity than we do.

## Nuclear Power Is Our Cheapest Source of Energy

Here's where the threat to our economy comes in: Nuclear power is considerably cheaper than any of the other common sources of energy. It's roughly one-half as expensive as coal, which is generally thought to be our cheapest fuel. And, nuclear power is even cheaper when compared with natural gas and oil.

**Table 1: The 1982 Cost of Electricity Generated by Nuclear Versus Coal**

| Fuel | Plant construction | Operating and Maintenance | Fuel | Total Cost per kilowatt hour |
|------|------|------|------|------|
| Nuclear | 0.92 | 0.50 | 0.82 | 2.24 cents |
| Coal | 1.11 | 0.42 | 2.80 | 4.33 cents |

Source: Commonwealth Edison, 1982.

The utility companies have carried out a lot of studies on the comparative costs of various fuels, and through the early 1980s almost all of them indicated that nuclear power was our cheapest fuel.

This table shows Commonwealth Edison's average operating costs for six large nuclear reactors and six comparable coal-fired power plants. It is worth noting that costs for plant construction and operating and maintenance were similar for both kinds of plants. But, fuel costs were over three times higher for the coal-fired plants. *Total cost per kilowatt hour, which is what counts, showed that electricity generated by coal-fired plants was almost twice as expensive as electricity produced by the nuclear power plants.*

Unfortunately, this picture has changed in the U.S. in recent years. In an attempt to placate the mobs of antinuclear activists and end the multitude of frivolous lawsuits they have filed, the Nuclear Regulatory Commission (NRC) has continually tightened regulations. Unfortunately, some of the new regulations haven't accomplished very much. For example, at one time regulations called for all welds to be x-rayed periodically so that a developing flaw could be detected long before the weld broke. This makes sense where pipes pass through metal containment, but it's an unnecessary, expensive bit of nonsense to have to x-ray the weld on a metal hand rail, which is what has to be done at nuclear power plants.

Unfortunately, none of these "improvements" was ever enough to satisfy the antinuclear activists. And, the NRC should have anticipated this. After all, the antinuclear activists were never interested in improving the safety of nuclear power plants; they have always been bent on stopping them from operating, no matter how safe they are.

Over the years, these regulatory changes have increased the cost of nuclear power plants, and they are now over twice as expensive to build in the U.S. as they are elsewhere.

When the antinuclear activists use the argument "nuclear power plants are too expensive to build," a bitter irony emerges. Nuclear power plants cost the same, or less, to build than coal-burning plants until the antinuclear activists forced construction costs up by filing hundreds of frivolous lawsuits and picketing.

## The Rest of the World Now Leads the War

Common sense proof of the comparative costs of producing energy using coal and nuclear power plants is provided by the former Eastern Bloc countries: By 1990 these countries had built 63 nuclear power plants, despite the fact that they hold some of the world's largest coal reserves. If nuclear power was more expensive than coal, why would these countries build even one nuclear plant?

When newly-elected President [Bill] Clinton outlined his plans for an energy tax in February of 1993, *energy industry figures showed that to produce a million BTUs of energy cost 50 cents if the energy was produced by nuclear power. But, coal costs were $1.10; natural gas, $2.40; and oil, $2.65 per million BTUs.* So, as a result of the antinuclear activists' work, although the energy produced by nuclear power plants was only from one-half to one-fifth as expensive as that produced by fossil fuels, we weren't building any more nuclear power plants.

But, the rest of the world was building nuclear power plants. Table 2 shows the percentage of electricity supplied by nuclear power in a number of countries.

It is sad to note that although we were once a leader in the use of nuclear power, we now lag badly behind other nations. In fact, a number of once less technically advanced nations have long since passed us by. And, there's a lot of danger in letting this happen. For example, in 1996, South Korea used cheap nuclear power to supply 36 percent of its electricity, while we generated only 22 percent of our electricity with nuclear power.

We have to compete in the world marketplace with South Korea. And, as you probably know, South Koreans will work for a whole lot less money than U.S. factory workers are happy with. So, not only will South Korea's energy costs be less, but their labor costs will also be less. This means that South Korean automobiles, computers, televisions, and other products will be significantly cheaper than those produced in the U.S. Nor are the South Koreans turning out junk—the quality of many of their products is just as good as ours. You have probably seen some of them— Gold Star television sets, Leading Edge computers, and Hyundai automobiles are examples of Korean products which have sold well in the U.S.

## How to Become a Second-Class Nation

Of course, if a Gold Star television set is just as good and significantly cheaper than a comparable U.S.-made set, the U.S. public will probably buy the Gold Star. At least, that's what has happened

## Table 2: The Percentage of Electrical Power Generated by Nuclear Power Plants in Various Countries

Note that there are a large number of countries (which many economists think are not as technologically advanced as the U.S.) that are using cheaper, healthier nuclear power to generate a larger percentage of their electricity than we do.

| Country | Percentage |
| --- | --- |
| Lithuania | 83.44% |
| France | 77.36% |
| Belgium | 57.18% |
| Sweden | 52.38% |
| Slovakia | 44.53% |
| Switzerland | 44.45% |
| Ukraine | 43.76% |
| Bulgaria | 42.24% |
| Hungary | 40.76% |
| Slovenia | 37.87% |
| Armenia | 36.72% |
| South Korea | 35.77% |
| Japan | 33.99% |
| Spain | 31.97% |
| Germany | 30.29% |
| Taiwan | 29.07% |
| Finland | 28.13% |
| United Kingdom | 26.04% |
| United States | 21.92% |

(Not shown: The twelve nations which use an even lower percentage of nuclear energy than the U.S.)

(Figures are for 1996, and are from the 1998 World Almanac.)

with other products: The U.S. now imports 100 percent of its table radios and VCRs. And, we import 85 percent of the black and white TVs sold here, and 68 percent of the digital watches. Less expensive foreign products have all but crowded us out of the market for these goods. The reason that we no longer manufacture table radios and VCRs in the U.S. is that we can't make one which is price competitive in the world market place. And, whenever this happens, we lose manufacturing plants and tens of thousands of jobs. Our labor and energy costs are so high that we are no longer competitive in an increasing number of areas.

Thirty-two years ago, in 1968, our Gross Domestic Product (GDP) per person was the highest in the world. Only eleven years later, we had fallen to eighth place. After that, things stabilized a bit, but by 1990, Switzerland's GDP per person was almost 50 percent higher than the U.S.'s. If this downward trend continues, a number of nations could have a much higher standard of living than we do before too many decades pass.

The word "sabotage" originated with the European Luddites who once dropped wooden shoes—"sabots"—into machinery in an attempt to destroy it. Today, the modern Luddites are sabotaging our attempts to remain economically competitive. But, they aren't dropping wooden shoes into the machinery any more. Instead, they are stopping us from building nuclear power plants, which are our cheapest, best source of energy.

# Terrorist Attacks on Nuclear Power Plants Are Possible

**By Friedrich Steinhausler**

Since September 11, 2001, terrorism has been at the forefront of many American and international minds. Terrorist scenarios often involve the use of radioactive materials, for example, in generating nuclear weapons (weapons of mass destruction), or less-sophisticated "dirty bombs." Other scenarios involve direct attacks on nuclear power plants. In the following selection, Friedrich Steinhausler considers what it would take for terrorists to attack a nuclear power plant. Steinhausler is an arms control expert at the Center for International Security and Cooperation at Stanford University.

There are 434 operating nuclear power plants (NPPs) worldwide. Due to their radioactive inventory (in the reactor core, in the spent fuel storage area, to a lesser extent in the fresh fuel depot), they represent an attractive target for a terrorist attack for the following reasons: instilling fear in the public about an uncontrolled release of radioactivity by merely threatening with the possibility of such an attack . . . and conducting an actual terrorist attack on vital areas of an operating nuclear power plant to inflict major damages to the facility, resulting in the loss of control over the plant. This could lead to major radioactive releases into the environment, resulting in elevated health risks and substantial economic losses for society.

In the recent past, such threats have occurred already in the United States and in Russia. However, so far, in all cases, the individuals could be neutralized in time by the respective national security forces.

# Protecting Against Security Risks

Security risks at NPPs can result from terrorists intruding onto the site of the NPP and through sabotage carried out by insiders. To manage such security risks, major efforts are undertaken by nuclear regulators, NPP operators, and managers to provide adequate physical protection for NPPs worldwide.

The protection against intruders consists typically of a series of fences, CCTV [closed-circuit television], cameras installed on site and at the site perimeter, as well as inspections of all persons and vehicles entering the site. In many countries, the basis for the specific security features is the *Design Basis Threat*, developed specifically for each NPP. This Design Basis Threat specifies the number of attackers to be assumed, together with the type of vehicle and weapons used in the attack, as well as the kind of assistance provided by the collaborating insider.

The protection against insiders is based on criminal background checks and psychological tests of employees.

Mock attacks on NPPs are carried out in the United States to test the state of readiness of the on-site security forces. However, despite preannouncement of the exercises, guards at half the nation's NPPs failed to repel the attackers.

# Sophisticated Terrorists

Terrorists can seriously threaten the security of an NPP in several manners, for example:

- *Attack mode no. 1:* A heavily armed suicide commando attacks the weakest entry point of an NPP with a truck bomb, followed by additional truck bombs breaking through the damaged barriers. This latter group attacks vital installations of the NPP.
- *Attack mode no. 2:* A suicide commando hijacks a fully fueled large aircraft and crashes it into the spent nuclear fuel storage area of the NPP.

The logistical and technical requirements are such that they are not within the realm of possibility of the average terrorist group but require a certain degree of sophistication. In particular, it would be necessary for this group to foresee that at least some of the members are prepared to die during the attack. Under these conditions, both attack modes could be successful, provided the terrorists succeed in acquisition of heavy weapons and a sufficient amount of explosives to build several truck bombs; obtain detailed knowledge about the layout of the NPP, the location of its vital components, and important plant-specific operational character-istics; succeed in hijacking a large civilian airliner; and inflict suf-ficient damage to the rather small cross section of vital NPP com-ponents either by detonating the truck bombs or by crashing the plane into them.

For both attack modes, it cannot be excluded that—in case of a successful attack—the resulting uncontrolled releases of radioac-tivity will result in a significant threat to man and the environment. The exact magnitude of any health risks to employees and nearby residents (external and internal radiation exposure), as well as the economic losses to the NPP itself and adjacent areas (production loss in agriculture, clean-up costs, devaluation of property value), cannot be estimated without specific input data characterizing the circumstances of the attack and the resulting radioactive release.

# Nuclear Terrorism Is Overrated

**By Douglas M. Chapin et al.**

America's defense agencies and nuclear commissions have long considered the threat of nuclear terrorism. In the most probable scenarios, terrorists are presumed to attack nuclear plants themselves or nuclear waste containers that are in transit to disposal. Douglas M. Chapin and the other authors of the following article, however, believe the dangers of such scenarios are exaggerated. They argue that both transport containers and plant walls, for example, are rigorously tested and proven strong enough to repel explosions. Furthermore, the authors assert that even if a nuclear container or plant wall was breached, the danger of a radioactive leak would be minimal. The suggested impossibility of success of this type of terrorist attack reveals the authors' desire to send a strong message in support of nuclear power. Douglas M. Chapin and his colleagues who aided in drafting this article are all members of the National Academy of Engineering.

If you watch television or read repeated public statements of concern about nuclear power plants as terrorist targets, you would be justified in believing that spent nuclear fuel casks being shipped to Nevada for storage are each a nuclear catastrophe just waiting to be triggered. These casks have been called "mobile Chernobyls," and we are told they are capable of causing "tens of thousands of deaths." What are the facts about the safety of nuclear shipments and power plants?

Since 11 September 2001, the U.S. nuclear industry and its regulators have been reevaluating plant and fuel shipment safety. These studies are being kept secret. But it is no secret that basic engineering facts and laws of nature limit the damage that can result. Extensive analysis, backed by full-scale field tests, show that there is virtually nothing one could do to these shipping casks that would cause a significant public hazard. Before shipment, the fuel elements have been cooled for several years, so the decay heat and the short-lived radioactivity have died down. They cannot explode, and there is no liquid radioactivity to leak out. They are nearly indestructible, having been tested against collisions, explosives, fire, and water. Only the latest antitank artillery could breach them, and then, the result was to scatter a few chunks of spent fuel onto the ground. There seems to be no reason to expect harmful effects of the radiation any significant distance from the cask.

## Possibility of a Meltdown

Similarly, we read that airplanes can fly through the reinforced, steel-lined 1.5-m-thick concrete walls surrounding a nuclear reactor and inevitably cause a meltdown resulting in "tens of thousands of deaths" and "make a huge area of the U.S. uninhabitable for centuries," to quote some recent stories. However, there seems to be no credible way to achieve that result. No airplane, regardless of size, can fly through such a wall. This has been calculated in detail and tested in 1988 by flying an unmanned plane at 215 m/s (about 480 mph) into a test wall 3.6 m thick. The plane, including its fuel tanks, collapsed against the outside of the wall, penetrating a few centimeters. The engines were a better penetrator, but still dug in only 5 cm. Analyses show that larger planes fully offset their greater impact by absorbing more energy during their collapse. Higher speed increases the impact, but not enough to matter. And inside the containment wall are additional walls of concrete and steel protecting the reactor.

Is it possible to cause a nuclear reactor to melt down some other way? Yes, it happened at Three Mile Island (TMI) in 1979. Reactors are much improved since then, and the probability of such an accident is now much less. But suppose it happens, through terrorist action or other; what then? Well, the TMI meltdown caused no significant environmental degradation or increased injury to any person, not even to the plant operators who stayed on duty. It has been said that this lack of public impact was due primarily to the containment structure. But studies after the accident showed that nearly all of the harmful fission products dissolved in the water and condensed out on the inside containment surfaces. Even if containment had been severely breached, little radioactivity would have escaped. Few, if any, persons would have been harmed.

To test how far the 10 to 20 metric tons of molten reactor penetrated the 13-cm-thick bottom of the reactor vessel on which it rested, samples were machined out of the vessel and examined. The molten mass did not even fully penetrate the 0.5-cm cladding, confirming tests in Karlsruhe, Germany, and in Idaho, that the "China syndrome"[1] is not a credible possibility.

The accident at Chernobyl in 1986 is simply not applicable to American reactors. The burning graphite dispersed most of the fission products directly into the atmosphere. Even in that situation, with no evacuation for several days, the United Nations' carefully documented investigation UN SCEAR-2000 reported that there were 30 deaths to plant operators and firefighters, but no significant increase in mortality or cancer due to irradiation of the public have been observed. A possible link between exposure and thyroid cancer is still under study. The terrible and widespread consequences of that accident—increased suicide, alcoholism, depression, and unemployment, plus 100,000 unnecessary abortions—were caused primarily by fear of radiation and by poor planning based on that fear. The evacuated lands are generally now no more radioactive than the natural background levels where many people have lived healthily for generations.

## Fear of Radiation

It's not surprising that some people overstate the concern about radiation, for whatever reason. But it is surprising that most nuclear advocates are reluctant to challenge such claims. They say they just want to be cautious. But striving for maximum caution leads to the assertion that we should act as if even the tiniest amount of radiation might be harmful, despite the large body of good scientific evidence that it is not. This policy has scared people away from mammograms and other life-saving treatments and has caused many Americans to die each year from pathogens that could have been killed by food irradiation. It has piled regulations on nuclear medicine facilities that caused many of them to

1. a hypothetical scenario where a reactor core melts, sinks into the earth, and travels all the way to China

shut down. And now, "permissible doses" have been pushed below those found in natural radiation backgrounds.

Such cautiousness has drawbacks when applied to design and operation of nuclear facilities. But it is particularly dangerous when applied to terrorism. To tell people that they and the Earth are in mortal danger from events that cannot cause significant public harm is to play into the hands of terrorists by making a minor event a cause for life-endangering panic. Now is the time to clear the air and speak a few simple scientific and engineering truths.

# CHRONOLOGY

**1895**

German physicist Wilhelm Röntgen discovers X-rays.

**1896**

French physicist Antoine-Henri Becquerel investigates the relationship between X-rays and visible light. By accident, he discovers that uranium emits mysterious rays even without exposure to light.

**1898**

Marie Curie, working with her husband, Pierre, studies Becquerel's mysterious rays and discovers that the element thorium also emits such rays. She coins the term "radioactivity" and discovers two new radioactive elements, polonium and radium.

**1899**

New Zealand–born physicist Ernest Rutherford discovers that uranium radiation contains two different kinds of rays: alpha rays, which are positively charged, and beta rays, which are negatively charged.

**1900**

French physicist Paul Villard discovers a third kind of ray emitted in radiation: gamma rays. These are even stronger than alpha and beta rays and do not carry an electrical charge.

**1911**

Ernest Rutherford discovers the atomic nucleus.

**1932**

British physicist James Chadwick discovers the neutron, a neutrally charged particle that exists along with protons inside the nucleus of an atom. Because of its neutral charge, researchers will soon discover that the neutron can serve as a projectile to bombard an atomic nucleus and initiate a nuclear reaction.

## 1934

Italian physicist Enrico Fermi discovers that "slow neutrons," or low-energy neutrons, are more efficient at starting nuclear reactions than more energetic neutrons. He achieves the first fission reaction, though he does not realize it at the time. In London, Hungarian physicist-in-exile Leo Szilard proposes the idea of a nuclear chain reaction.

## 1938

Austrian physicist Lise Meitner, in exile in Sweden, and nephew Otto Frisch study the splitting of uranium atoms by German physicists Otto Hahn and Fritz Strassman. Meitner and Frisch coin the term "fission" to describe how uranium, when bombarded, splits into two smaller elements.

## 1939

More than one hundred articles on fission are published in scientific journals. On August 2 German physicist Albert Einstein, in exile in the United States, sends a letter to President Franklin D. Roosevelt informing him of the possibility that nuclear chain reactions can be used to produce very powerful bombs.

## 1942

Roosevelt authorizes the top-secret Manhattan Project, involving the best and brightest scientists in the country in an all-out effort to build an atomic bomb. On December 2, in a squash court under Stagg Field at the University of Chicago, Enrico Fermi and colleagues generate the first controlled, sustained nuclear chain reaction.

## 1945

In August the United States drops atomic bombs on the Japanese cities of Hiroshima and Nagasaki, bringing World War II to an end.

## 1946

Congress passes the Atomic Energy Act, authorizing the establishment of the Atomic Energy Commission to encourage and regulate the atomic energy industry.

## 1953

The Atomic Energy Commission and Duquesne Light Company announce plans to build a 60 MWe (megawatts electric) nuclear power plant in Shippingport, Pennsylvania. On December 8 President Dwight D. Eisenhower gives a speech, known as "Atoms for Peace," to the American people, in which he urges countries to use atomic energy for peaceful means rather than for warfare.

## 1954

A small, experimental nuclear reactor, the 5 MWe Obninsk Atomic Energy Station, begins generating electricity in the Soviet Union on June 27.

## 1956

The British nuclear reactor, 50 MWe Calder Hall, begins operating on October 17.

## 1957

The Shippingport nuclear reactor goes into operation. It is the first commercial reactor in the United States, producing sixty megawatts of power. Eisenhower signs the Price-Anderson Act into law, giving electric utilities protection from liability in the event of a power plant accident.

## 1959

The Dresden 1 Nuclear Power Station in Illinois goes online. It is the first nuclear power plant in the United States to be built without any government funding.

## 1962

Four more nuclear power plants are completed in the United States.

## 1968

Seventy-five nuclear power plants are in various stages of planning, design, and construction. Most become operational within the decade.

## 1970

Construction of the Chernobyl nuclear power plant begins in the Ukraine, then part of the Soviet Union.

## 1974

The Energy Reorganization Act abolishes the Atomic Energy Commission, replacing it with the Energy Research and Development Administration and the Nuclear Regulatory Commission.

## 1977

The Energy Research and Development Administration becomes part of the Department of Energy.

## 1978

The last two new nuclear power plants are ordered in the United States.

## 1979

The worst nuclear power plant accident in United States history occurs on March 28 at the Three Mile Island Unit 2 nuclear power plant near Harrisburg, Pennsylvania. No one is killed. Thousands in the surrounding community are evacuated.

## 1986

The worst nuclear power plant in world history occurs on April 25 at the Chernobyl power plant in the Ukraine. More than thirty people die in the fires that ensue. Hundreds of thousands are evacuated.

## 1996

The last new nuclear power plant in the United States goes online at Watts Barr, Tennessee.

# FOR FURTHER RESEARCH

## Books

Stephen A. Atkins, *Historical Encyclopedia of Atomic Energy.* Westport, CT: Greenwood, 2000.

William Beaver, *Nuclear Power Goes On-line: A History of Shippingport.* New York: Greenwood, 1990.

Petr Beckman, *The Health Hazards of Not Going Nuclear.* Boulder, CO: Golem, 1976.

Irvin C. Bupp and Jean-Claude Derian, *Light Water: How the Nuclear Dream Dissolved.* New York: Basic Books, 1978.

John L. Campbell, *Collapse of an Industry: Nuclear Power and the Contradictions of U.S. Policy.* Ithaca, NY: Cornell University Press, 1988.

Philip L. Cantelon, Richard G. Hewlett, and Robert C. Williams, eds., *The American Atom: A Documentary History of Nuclear Policies from the Discovery of Fission to the Present.* Philadelphia: University of Pennsylvania Press, 1991.

Philip L. Cantelon and Robert C. Williams, *Crisis Contained: The Department of Energy at Three Mile Island.* Carbondale: Southern Illinois University Press, 1982.

Bernard L. Cohen, *Before It's Too Late: A Scientist's Case for Nuclear Power.* New York: Plenum, 1983.

——, *The Nuclear Energy Option: An Alternative for the 90s.* New York: Plenum, 1990.

Helen Cothran, ed., *Opposing Viewpoints: Energy Alternatives.* San Diego: Greenhaven, 2002.

Richard Wayne Dyke, *Mr. Atomic Energy: Congressman Chet Holifield and Atomic Energy Affairs, 1945–1974, Volume 241.* Westport, CT: Greenwood, 1989.

John Giacobello, *Nuclear Power of the Future: New Ways of Turning Atoms into Energy.* New York: Rosen, 2003.

Sidney Goodman, *Asleep at the Geiger Counter: Nuclear Destruction of the Planet and How to Stop It.* Nevada City, NV: Blue Dolphin, 2002.

Harry Henderson, *Nuclear Physics.* New York: Facts On File, 1998.

Margaret O. Hyde and Bruce G. Hyde, *Everyone's Trash Problem: Nuclear Wastes.* New York: McGraw-Hill, 1979.

J.S. Kidd and Renee A. Kidd, *Quarks and Sparks: The Story of Nuclear Power.* New York: Facts On File, 1999.

Amory B. Lovins and John H. Price, *Non-Nuclear Futures: The Case for an Ethical Energy Strategy.* San Francisco: Friends of the Earth International, 1975.

Joseph G. Morone and Edward J. Woodhouse, *The Demise of Nuclear Energy? Lessons for Democratic Control of Technology.* New Haven, CT: Yale University Press, 1989.

Thomas H. Moss and David S. Sills, *The Three Mile Island Nuclear Accident: Lessons and Implications.* New York: New York Academy of Sciences, 1981.

Raymond L. Murray, *Nuclear Energy.* New York: Pergamon, 1988.

——, *Understanding Radioactive Waste.* Columbus, OH: Battelle, 2003.

Adriana Petryna, *Life Exposed: Biological Citizens After Chernobyl.* Princeton, NJ: Princeton University Press, 2002.

Richard Rhodes, *Nuclear Renewal: Common Sense About Energy.* New York: Penguin, 1993.

*Scientific American, Energy for Planet Earth: Readings from* Scientific American Magazine. New York: W.H. Freeman, 1991.

Glenn Theodore Seaborg, with Benjamin S. Loeb, *The Atomic Energy Commission Under Nixon: Adjusting to Troubled Times.* New York: St. Martin's, 1993.

J. Samuel Walker, *Three Mile Island: A Nuclear Crisis in Histori-*

*cal Perspective.* Berkeley and Los Angeles: University of California Press, 2004.

# Periodicals

Dean Abrahamson and Johan Swahn, "The Political Atom," *Bulletin of the Atomic Scientists*, July 2000.

H.A. Bethe, "The Necessity of Fission Power," *Scientific American*, January 1976.

Michael Crowley, "On the Hill: Waste Away," *New Republic*, November 26, 2001.

*Ecologist*, "1942–2002: Sixty Years of Nuclear," December 2002.

*Economist*, "Fact and Fission; Energy Policy," July 19, 2003.

Bernard L. Cohen, "Perspectives on the Nuclear Debate," *Bulletin of the Atomic Scientists*, October 1974.

John Douglas, "Reopening the Nuclear Option," *EPRI Journal*, December 1994.

Ben Evans, "Nuclear Power 'Rebirth': Still Too Hot to Handle?" *CQ Weekly*, February 28, 2005.

Fritz Gautschi, "Nuclear Power Return May Hinge on Advanced Gas-Cooled Reactor Designs," *Power Engineering*, March 2003.

Sergei Kiselyov, Viktoria Tripolskaya-Mitlyng, and Astghik Vardanian, "Inside the Beast," *Bulletin of the Atomic Scientists*, May/June 1996.

Amory B. Lovins, "Energy Strategy: The Road Not Taken?" *Foreign Affairs*, October 1976.

Laura Maggi, "Making White Elephants Fly," *American Prospect*, February 28, 2000.

L.J. Nilsson and Dean E. Abrahamson, "Safeguarding and Internationalizing Nuclear Power," *International Journal of Global Energy Issues*, March 1991.

*Nuclear Engineering International*, "Skies Remain Cloudy for Nuclear Persuaders," April 2003.

Richard Rhodes and Denis Beller, "The Need for Nuclear Power," *Foreign Affairs*, January/February 2000.

Stanley Rothman and S. Robert Lichter, "The Nuclear Energy Debate: Scientists, the Media and the Public," *Public Opinion*, August/September 1982.

Robert N. Schock, Eileen S. Vergino, Neff Joeck, Ronald F. Lehman, "Atoms for Peace After 50 Years: President Eisenhower's Hopes for Nuclear Technology Still Resonate, but the Challenges of Fulfilling Them Are Much Different Today," *Issues in Science and Technology*, Spring 2004.

John J. Taylor, "The Nuclear Power Bargain: The Potential Benefits Are Enormous If We Can Continue to Make Progress on Safety, Environmental, Fuel Supply, and Proliferation Concerns," *Issues in Science and Technology*, Spring 2004.

Kirk Victor, "The Nuclear Turn-On," *National Journal*, September 9, 1989.

Alvin M. Weinberg, "The Moral Imperatives of Nuclear Energy," *Nuclear News*, December 1971.

## Internet Sources

Spurgeon M. Keeny Jr., "Plutonium Processing: Twenty Years Experience (1977–1997)," *Frontline*, 1997. www.pbs.org/wgbh/pages/frontline/shows/reaction/readings/keeny.html.

John McCarthy, "Frequently Asked Questions About Nuclear Energy," 1995. www-formal.stanford.edu/jmc/progress/nuclear-faq.html.

Jon Palfreman, "Why the French Like Nuclear Energy," *Frontline*, 1998. www.pbs.org/wgbh/pages/frontline/shows/reaction/readings/french.html.

*Seattle Times*, "Fifty Years from Trinity, Part III: Hanford Site," 1995. http://seattletimes.nwsource.com/trinity/articles/part3.html.

Uranium Information Centre, Ltd., "The Economics of Nuclear Power," April 2005. www.uic.com.au/nip08.htm.

# Web Sites

Nuclear Energy Institute, www.nei.org. The Nuclear Energy Institute is an organization that promotes and supports the atomic energy industry in public policy matters. Its members include companies that own nuclear power plants, design and engineering firms, and other companies and research institutions within the field of atomic energy. In addition to providing fact sheets, news, updates on public policy issues and technical information, the institute's Web site offers a "science club" that is open to all visitors. Within the science club, users can learn the history of nuclear energy, how atoms are split, and how nuclear power plants work, as well as gain insight into the industry's perspective on the benefits of atomic energy. It also offers numerous links to additional useful resources.

Nuclear Regulatory Commission, www.nrc.gov. The Nuclear Regulatory Commission (NRC) has a mission to regulate the nuclear industry to ensure public safety and well-being. They specifically regulate three areas: nuclear reactors, nuclear materials, and nuclear waste. The commission's Web site provides the latest information on proposed regulations, reactor licensing procedures, and power plants. It also offers a large array of full-text NRC documents.

Union of Concerned Scientists, www.ucsusa.org. According to its Web site, the Union of Concerned Scientists "is an independent nonprofit alliance of more than 100,000 concerned citizens and scientists" who "augment rigorous scientific analysis with innovative thinking and committed citizen advocacy to build a cleaner, healthier environment and a safer world." The site provides extensive analysis of nuclear safety issues as well as information about alternative energy resources.

# INDEX